May, 1986

For Carol and Bill —
on the anniversary
that special day —
as you continue to
celebrate your love —
Fondly, Mom & Dad E.

THE

Adolphus

COOKBOOK

THE
Adolphus
COOKBOOK

JOANNE SMITH

Cuisine Photography
by Don Heit

TAYLOR PUBLISHING COMPANY
Dallas, Texas

Copyright © 1983, Taylor Publishing Company
1550 West Mockingbird Lane, Dallas, Texas 75235

Library of Congress Cataloging in Publication Data

Smith, Joanne, 1931-
    The Adolphus cookbook.

    Includes index.
    1. Cookery, American — Texas. 2. Cookery, European.
3. Adolphus Hotel (Dallas, Tex.) 4. Dallas (Tex.) —
Social life and customs. 5. Dallas (Tex.) — Hotels,
motels, etc. I. Title.
TX715.S6626   1983   641.5′09764′2812   83-18018
ISBN 0-87833-339-8

Printed in the United States of America

To Adolphus A. Busch (1839-1913),
by whose champagne taste and beer-baron pocketbook
the Hotel Adolphus grew from dream to reality.

ACKNOWLEDGMENTS

With thanks to members of the Adolphus staff for their splendid cooperation, especially:

John B. Kirk, General Manager

Betty J. Holloway, Director of Public Relations

Jean Pierre Piallier, Pastry Chef

Michel Cornu, Executive Chef

Claude Feracci, Executive Sous Chef

Pascal Gode, French Room Chef

Pascal Vignau, French Room Chef

Tim Paige, Sous Chef, The Grille

Filbert Johnson, Banquet Chef,

and to Pat Scribner of Concepts Originale, who created the floral arrangements for the color photographs. Thanks and applause to food photographer Don Heit, and to Jack Lewis of *Texas Highways*, for exterior photographs of the building. Special thanks to all those whose memories, words, photographs and other memorabilia have added to the folkloric history of the hotel.

Foreword

In 1912, original investment in quality craftsmanship and service made the Hotel Adolphus unusually beautiful. Now, thanks to a complete outer restoration and inner renovation in 1981, we believe that its combined history, style and decor have boosted the old-world hotel into the rank of world-class. In Dallas, at least, the Adolphus imparts a different feeling, spiritually and physically, from any other quality hotel.

Shortly before the re-opening of the hotel, I accompanied the president of AMFAC to Europe for a close look at some of the traditional old hotels, particularly in London. We have tried to adapt the fine European standard of service we saw there to the warmth of Texas hospitality, generating a style of our own.

We are proud of our staff and believe that much of our hospitality comes from the chefs responsible for food services in the hotel. The recipe collection in this book welcomes you into our kitchen, whether you have visited the hotel or not, to take something of the Adolphus spirit home with you.

Enjoy!

John B. Kirk
General Manager
The Adolphus

Introduction

Tradition, legend and glamour have contributed to the
Adolphus mystique, but warm hospitality and essential good
taste remain at the base of the hotel's reputation. Since the re-
opening in 1981, the Adolphus' outstanding quality has been
underscored with the AAA 5-Diamond Award for all hospitality and services. The French Room has received consistent 5-
Star ratings in restaurant reviews, including the "Award for
Dining Distinction" from *TRAVEL/HOLIDAY's* Guide to Fine
Dining.

Much of the success of the hotel's dining services is due, no
doubt, to the right blend of personalities and selection of
employees who take pride in their work. A great deal of credit
for the hotel's standard of excellence, however, can be directed
to the original selection of menus and presentation of cuisine
established for the Adolphus food services by food consultant,
Jean Banchet.

The current staff of French chefs was trained by Banchet at
his own restaurant, Le Français, in Wheeling, Illinois. At least
once each month, Banchet comes to Dallas to maintain the
original standard and to offer solutions to any new problems.
"Even the smallest garnish is important," Banchet says,
"especially in the *nouvelle cuisine,* with its lighter sauces and
delicate balance of herbs and spices. Nothing should be
overlooked."

This collection of recipes presents some of the best of each
food service, divided according to each of the hotel's three
restaurants: The French Room, The Grille Restaurant, and The
Palm Bar. A fourth section gives recipes for stocks, dressings
and sauces; a fifth presents recipes from Afternoon Tea in the
lobby; a sixth takes you down to the heart of the matter, the
pastry kitchen. The final sections include tips for presenting
food attractively and recipes from the banquet kitchen.

A few dishes have many steps and, therefore, cannot be

prepared hurriedly, but most recipes will not seem difficult.

A prelude to the recipe collection explores the hotel's folkloric history. Over a seventy year span, many fond memories were born at the Adolphus. Some of these memories have been assembled to create a verbal mosaic of the hotel's history and traditions.

All recipes in this collection are authentic. They were prepared by the chefs for the color photographs by Don Heit. Remember, though, that the seasonings in any recipe must be regarded as recommended measurements. Feel free to take these with a grain of salt. And, please, use as much salt as you like on the story of the hotel.

I hope you enjoy reading about The Grand Dame and preparing some of the favorites from her kitchen as much as I have enjoyed researching and writing about it.

Joanne Smith
Dallas, Texas, 1983

Contents

The Adolphus Heritage

The towering Adolphus, with mansard roof and Beaux Arts styling, was spectacular on old Commerce Street in 1912.

When the graceful young Adolphus first raised her copper crowning glory against the drab 1912 skyline, Dallas gasped at the impact of her beauty. Entering the scene like an exotic debutante, the 21-story hotel demanded attention. Indeed, her architectural features fascinated all who saw them, even those who had never seen nor heard of the muses and deities keeping vigil beneath her rooftop. Predictably, the ingenue hotel soon grew into a symbol of Dallas hospitality, the center of social, political and special business events.

Dallas and the Adolphus have enjoyed the sort of long-standing romance that comes but once in a lifetime. As so often happens, the brilliance of that romance became worn into a soft patina, as the fiery copper crown mellowed into green, and the relationship settled into a taken-for-granted fact. Neither the affair nor the hotel itself fell into an irreversible state of disrepair, but both faded remotely into the city's background. Then, just when we seemed to have put the hotel's day of glory behind us, something happened to renew its life. Now, we are celebrating a new era.

A Seventy Year Legend

Beautiful Lady with a Past. Grande Dame. Queen Mother. A litany of romantic metaphors has likened the Adolphus to a gracious aristocrat recovering her lost fortune, and has praised her as a great actress making her second debut. Her self-renewal has even been compared to the ever-arising phoenix. Whatever her image, in the more than seventy years she and Dallas have been together, the bond seems stronger now than ever.

When you ask several people who have known an aging actress to describe her, their answers will vary according to the time and role in which they knew her best. One might remember the Grande Dame as a young, effervescent beauty, with more promise than actual delivery of a great performance; another might recall great talent combined with classical grandeur; in middle age, her queenly demeanor may have been seasoned with a relaxed sense of humor and a slightly raucous kind of laughter. Several generations of college students know her best as the center of the Friday-night revelry on Texas-OU weekend.

Wholesale markets, entertainment, professional clubs and special events were all part of her act. Whether the Adolphus is characterized as an actress or simply as an outstanding hotel, her legend, like her beauty, is still being defined within the eye of each beholder.

* * *

In 1912, the size of the Adolphus was even more striking than the sunlight bouncing off the roof. By comparison, everything else on the horizon seemed dwarfed and provincial. The beautiful new hotel established owner Adolphus A. Busch in Dallas as a man of both means and good taste.

Some have questioned the Anheuser-Busch President's motives for building the landmark hotel in Dallas, suggesting that it might have been a goodwill gesture connected with beer sales. Whether this notion has any basis or not, the people of Dallas extended a warm and enthusiastic welcome to both beer and hotel. Others have suggested that political interests prompted investment in the economy of Dallas, having some hazy connection with diverting the course of oncoming Prohibition. Probably not. Prohibition was still several years away.

Busch was no stranger to the area and, in 1893, when completion of the Oriental Hotel was delayed for lack of funds, he had come to the rescue with financial support. According to a narrative by Elise Mitchell, researched for the Dallas County Historical Commission, Adolphus Busch was approached about building a new hotel by representatives of the Dallas Chamber of Commerce:

"Charles F. Bolanz, Henry Lindsay and S.J. Hay went to St. Louis to induce Adolphus Busch to build a first rate hotel in Dallas. In May 1910, Busch wrote to S.J. Hay stating his intention to buy downtown property and build a hotel on it. Busch purchased land from Mrs. M.G. Starke, her husband Neal Starke and from the City of Dallas in 1911. The Hotel Adolphus was constructed on the site of the 1880's Dallas City Hall, at the corner of Commerce and Akard Streets, for an original cost of $1,870,000."

Busch went to great expense and trouble to build a first class hotel. Architects Barnett, Haynes and Barnett designed the building in the style of the *Ecole de Beaux Arts,* with a bronze and slate mansard roof and a facade decorated with French Renaissance features in relief. Three dimensional carvings included floral and animal figures as well as full figures and figureheads, mainly on the south (Commerce Street) side and the east (Akard Street) side. Where the two sides were joined a turret resembling a bottle adorned the roof. From its granite base, up the red brick shaft, all the way to its striking capital features, every detail was given the best possible attention. The results were breathtaking. Adolphus Busch must have been pleased — he named the hotel after himself. The Dallas

Busch's Hotel Helped Shape Dallas History

Chamber of Commerce showed its appreciation by naming Busch an honorary member.

Sometime after Busch's death, his heirs expanded the size of the hotel. The first annex, built by Lang and Witchell, appeared in 1918, unattached, but connected by a walkway to the original hotel. Further additions came in 1926, under Busch family ownership, and, again, in 1951, after Leo Corrigan had bought the hotel. After a series of other additions (only some of which were improvements), the hotel was completely air-conditioned in 1945, and fitted with Otis autotronic elevators. The number of rooms had skyrocketed to a peak 1,370 rooms, with some the result of simple, ill-advised long division. Later, the rooms were enlarged somewhat, with the number of rooms cut. In 1980, under completely new ownership, the hotel was completely renovated for its second debut.

On May 4, 1981, the Adolphus was listed in the National Register of Historic Places. In September of that same year, when the hotel reopened, the Texas Historical Commission placed its official, Texas-shaped marker on the building:

Lights, paneling, and massive spaces gave the hotel lobby a feeling of grandeur.

ADOLPHUS HOTEL
Dallas businessmen persuaded Adolphus Busch (1839-1913), co-founder of the Anheuser Busch Brewing Co., to build the original section of this hotel in 1911-1912. Constructed on the site of the 1880s Dallas City Hall and designed by the St. Louis firm of Barnett, Haynes and Barnett, it features *Beaux Arts* styling with elaborate French Renaissance detailing. For years Dallas' skyline was dominated by the Adolphus, the scene of many important business and social events. Recorded Texas Historic Landmark — 1981.

In 1982, the American Institute of Architects presented their Honor Award to Beran and Shelmire in recognition of outstanding achievement in the renovation of the Adolphus Hotel.

* * *

German-born Adolphus A. Busch accomplished so much in his lifetime that he probably considered building a 21-story hotel a minor achievement. Perhaps twenty-one was Busch's favorite number. He was the youngest of twenty-one children born to Ulrich and Barbara Pfeifer Busch. He was twenty-one years old when he married Lilly Anheuser in St. Louis. Busch could have designated the twenty-first floor Skyway Suite to be his home away from St. Louis, but, he also divided his time among several other homes: one in Pasadena, California; another in Cooperstown, New York; and, the apparent

Busch was still a European aristocrat, as this stately portrait reveals.

favorite, a villa at Langen-schwalbach, in his native Germany. Busch spent more time there than anywhere else during his last years, and died there on October 13, 1913, just one year after the Adolphus opened.

The original Adolphus Hotel building bears witness to the taste of Adolphus Busch as well as to his obvious tendency to seek out the finest in arts and craftsmanship. Less well-known in the Dallas area, but another manifestation of Busch's feeling for luxury class, is the private stable he built in St. Louis in 1885, now used for the famous Clydesdale horses. An early press release describes the stable as "An equine palace all horse lovers should visit." The equine palace probably bore some resemblance to the contemporary stables of European royalty.

The press release maintains that "Adolphus Busch was not a sporting man or fast stock fancier; his fondness for horses was based on the nobility, intelligence, patience, amiability and affectionate characteristics of the animal, rather than its powers of motion." The stable was presented as "The very handsomest architectural feature among all the costly buildings that cover the forty-seven blocks of brewery property."

The press release goes on to explain Mr. Busch's theory that such a clean, orderly, non-destructive animal should be housed as comfortably as a human being. Toward this end, he executed the building of an octagonal brick stable, 95 x 110 feet, which made many human beings' houses seem poor by comparison. Built in 1885 at a cost of $35,000, the stable was lighted with electricity and heated with steam, among other luxury features. A description of the carriage, waiting and billiard rooms, and the superintendent's office, as well as the washrooms and the stable proper, mentions hardwood panels, clay and wooden floors, cement, enameled brick wainscoating and polished stone bases, along with ornamental iron guards, marble top basins, earthenware sinks, and "cathedral glass of variegated hues."

Busch honored both the equine palace and his namesake hotel with a signature of sorts: twin circular chandeliers, featuring gilt eagles and hops, which he had bought from the French Pavilion at the 1904 St. Louis World Fair. A ring of knobs, reminiscent of a horsecollar, at the top of each chandelier, familiar hops, and eagles similar to the registered Anheuser-Busch logo (1877) lead many to believe that Busch commissioned their design. Not so, say the Anheuser-Busch archives; he saw the massive fixtures and bought them. Possibly, however, the designer of the large metal chandeliers had Adolphus Busch in mind for their purchase.

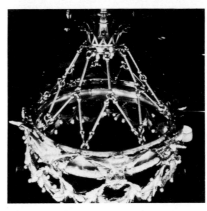

The ornate chandelier still adorns the hotel lobby.

*   *   *

On October 5, 1912, *The Dallas Morning News* announced the formal opening of the hotel, stating that the manager, A. Wilson, "and his corps of expert assistants" had perfected all preliminary details and anticipated "every success to be attendant upon their plans for the day." The management promised that the Adolphus spirit and the Adolphus service would be "Thoroughly in evidence in all the procedures of the opening day ... these being the terms by which Manager Wilson expresses the high standard which he has established as the characteristics of the hostelry ..." The stockholders' inspection would be conducted with card-only admittance, followed by an informal reception in the Palm Garden and a buffet luncheon. Some of the stockholders were described as "a party of St. Louis Capitalists," arriving in the private car, *Adolphus,* of course, to participate in the event.

On the same October day, Titche-Goettinger Company's advertisement saluted "a great stride in the progress of this city." According to the Titche's ad, "This hotel was furnished from pit to dome by the different business houses of this city. Some furnished the furniture, others the floor covering, others the linens, towels, bedding, etc. The Adolphus stands as a monument to home buying . . . reciprocity in its simplest yet very highest term."

* * *

From the beginning, the hotel was the scene of major social events. Mrs. Samuel A. Shelburne, nee Gertrude Aldredge, still remembers the excitement of the first big event she attended in her early childhood: "In the springtime of 1914, Uncle Sawnie Aldredge, who later became Mayor of Dallas, brought his bride Mary Batts to this city. The family held a big reception at the Adolphus to introduce her to society," she says. "I remember the occasion, even my lacy, white dress. I was a very young child, still small enough that someone carried me through the door." It made a lasting impression. "It was beautiful," she says.

By the time young Gertrude Aldredge made her debut at the Idlewild Ball in October of 1929, two additions had enlarged the hotel. They probably detracted from its charm, aesthetically, but the additions allowed the Hotel Adolphus to absorb more and more of the Dallas social life. It was chic to talk about Peacock Alley, and the roof garden, where big windows promised some breeze, at least, to dancers on warm evenings. All agreed that it was a ritzy place to dine and dance.

Though less appealing, the newer additions helped to accommodate the hotel's growing business.

Mrs. Shelburne recalls her debut: "I still preferred white, but my mother asked me to save the white for my own ball (which, incidentally, was scheduled for the also-ritzy Crystal Ballroom of the Baker Hotel, across the street). My gown was a pale blue brocade, multi-tiered with flounces. Of course, it was a designer gown, ordered by Neiman-Marcus from New York," she says.

"There was no court bow then; we were simply presented. My escort was Albert Sidney Johnson, the president of Idlewild." What happened after the presentation? "Everyone seemed to have disappeared for a time," she says with a smile. "I thought they had all gone home. It turned out that nearly

Early postcards revealed the frontier quality of the city when Adolphus Busch first came to Dallas.

everyone attending the ball also had a private room to enjoy Prohibition-type cocktails, in a plain brown wrapper. But they all came back."

Yet another Aldredge generation enjoyed the hospitality of the Adolphus. "In 1952," says Mrs. Shelburne, "my niece's wedding rehearsal dinner was held in one of the private dining rooms."

When Mrs. Shelburne's friend, Georgia Cary Brower, made her debut at the Idlewild of 1932, she felt right at home. And, rightly so. Her grandmother, Mrs. Jules Schneider, lived at the Adolphus. Looking back at the Twenties, Mrs. Brower says, "As a very young girl, my idea of heaven was to spend the night with my grandmother at the hotel." It was a dream castle to the little girl, and she was the princess.

Another lady who lived in the Adolphus in the early days was the widowed Lena Cox Wren, who died there as well. She

The Adolphus

Dallas, Texas.

Popular
With
Motorists.

Rooms, $1.50 up.

Club Breakfasts.

R. B. Ellifritz,
Manager.

Even with room rates at $1.50, the Adolphus attracted the carriage trade, as this colorful postcard suggests.

must have been very sentimental about the hotel; among her things were picture post cards of the hotel and its lobby. One of the cards she saved, dated 1916, named R.B. Ellifritz, Manager. It shows an open motor car driven by a George Washington look-alike, a friend, and two ladies dressed like Martha. "Popular with Motorists," the card says, "Rooms, $1.50 up. Club Breakfasts."

If $1.50 per room seems a bargain, consider the seven-course lunch available at the hotel's Bambooland in the good old days. The menu offered a choice of at least six dishes in each category. Featured were Crabmeat Canape Moderne; Cream of Quail Luculus; Escaloppe of Veal Saute au Beurre with New String Beans Menagere; Baked Summer Squash Princesse with Asparagus Tips; Baked Potatoes au Gratin; Salad Elsinore, Green Dressing; with Fresh Fruit Tartlet for dessert. Don't forget the Loganberry Iced Tea. All for 75¢.

"Both noon and night," the menu boasted "special entertainment features and music are provided for our patrons . . . Cabaret and Orchestrations of the finest selection and rendition. Dancing may be enjoyed by those desiring to participate. Also, patrons may remain for the Regular Dance without extra charge." And, by the way, "No Cover Charge."

Foster Prather remembers Bambooland in 1920. He came to Dallas to celebrate June 19th, and, while he was celebrating, his auntie's brother-in-law got him a busboy job at Bambooland. "75¢ doesn't sound like much now," he says, "But, when I was 16, a dollar a day was a lot of money to me; that's what I made running the elevator at Neiman-Marcus." When was that? "I don't know the year, but Mr. Stanley (Marcus) was at a boys' school."

"In Bambooland, though, we served in the main dining room till 9:00, until the dancing started. Then, hot food had to be served on the other side of the roof. We did room service, too, but we carried the tables on our shoulders, not on wheels. I used to help Mr. Barbosa carry those when people ordered big things on Saturday night." There was no problem on Sunday morning: "All they wanted was canned tomatoes with Worcestershire to take care of corn liquor hangovers."

When the roof garden closed for the winter, in September, the main dining room (where the French Room is now) opened. "It was first-class," Prather says, "with snowy white linens and great big napkins. The head waiter trained me to be a waiter then, and I had my own table for four plus-one table for two. Each of us took care of just that much, and whatever they ordered, such as Chicken a la King, we mixed it at the table."

Sheet music for "Dallas, I Love You," with scenes of the famed hotel.

There was always entertainment; Prather saw Valentino dance in the Junior Ballroom. "That room was packed with ladies," he says, "and we were supposed to serve tea at $5 a plate. But once he started to dance, we all just watched." Probably the ladies didn't even notice the lapse of service. "Caruso came once, but not to sing. He ordered spaghetti and had me bring everything to the table for him to mix it himself."

"We did a lot of things for people," he says. "Sometimes people would bring ducks back from hunting and we fixed them. All they ate then was the breast, so everything else was put into the duck presser and the juice squeezed out to make a sauce. I should say it was good . . ."

At that time, the music was broadcast on WRR. "Trent's Orchestra, all black, played in the roof garden," says Prather. "They broadcast at 11:00 P.M., from the roof garden or the Junior Ballroom. All the girls in my neighborhood were crazy about him."

A mysterious duet came from the Adolphus studio, too. A picture in the *Dallas Times Herald* showed the "Mystery Singers," complete with guitar, banjo and face masks. Their names were never given. Billed as "neither here nor there," they were said to "haunt" the studio at 5:00 P.M. each Wednesday.

* * *

Beyond a doubt, the early Adolphus menu had class. On February 6, 1920, after General Pershing reviewed parade troops from above the porte cochere, his party retreated to the dining room to feast upon *Isle of Pine Grapefruit Maraschino, Celery, Olives, Salted Almonds; Pot au Feu Polonaise, Pailette d'Or; Poitrine de Poulette Sauté, Legion d'Honor; Pommes Dauphinoise; Salade d'Asparagus Française; Mousse aux Pistachio; Mignardise de Patisserie* and *Cafe Noir*.

Colonel Henry D. Lindsley was Toastmaster, followed by Mayor Frank W. Wozencraft in a welcoming address. Major Arch Allen represented the American Legion, and the well-known Baptist minister, Reverend George W. Truett, delivered some uplifting thoughts. The response came from General John J. "Blackjack" Pershing himself.

The Adolphus must have pioneered the art of seeking out genuine, European-trained chefs and attracting them to the great Southwest. Such chefs were hard to come by in 1922, and to complicate matters further, if one of them moved on, the whole crew followed. Sometimes, however, that fact worked in the hotel's favor. Certainly, it did when a Belgian Chef Patissier, Prosper A. Ingels, followed his chef-brother Jerome to Dallas and joined the Adolphus staff. He remained in charge of the pastry kitchen for forty-eight years, until his retirement in 1970.

The heat in the kitchen was unbearable, according to Prosper Ingels, with all ovens fired, and, as the cliche goes, he tried to get out of it. "Three times I quit, just in the first year," he laughs, "but they gave me a raise each time, so I came back." Ingels was worth the price. During the 48-year era, Prosper's pastry kitchen became famous for incredible ice sculpture and pulled-sugar works of art, as well as for the always-crisp French bread rolls and pastry delights. His whole wheat apple pie alone could have made him famous. Everyone who ever tasted it still remembers how good it was.

Undoubtedly, Ingels was the only real, third-generation pastry chef in town in those days. His background qualified him to know all about Belgian hospitality. Even now, his family in Belgium still owns and manages a summer resort on the North Sea.

Besides baking beautiful bread and pastry, the talented Ingels sculpted anything and everything to order. At the Republic Bank's opening, each of 52 tables had its own icy bank building. For the automobile show, four ice-elephants twirled on a stand holding a Chevrolet on top (although few took any notice of the Chevy). Corrigan once ordered a large ice lioness with four nursing cubs. The English wanted battleships; someone else wanted a swan; Texas vs. Oklahoma week-end buffets warranted covered wagons, cowboys, Indians and Longhorns. Jack Benny appeared at the Pan

*Prosper Ingels'
pastry kitchen
turned out works of
art for all occasions.*

American Exposition in 1937 (when he may have been actually 39-years-old); in his honor, Ingels fashioned a sparkling ice-and-jello violin. Very fitting, as was the candy replica of the Spirit of St. Louis which Ingels had made ten years before when Lindbergh came to the hotel. And the chef fashioned a colorful bust of Franklin D. Roosevelt to crown the President's birthday cake.

"Pulled sugar is the real test of a chef patissier," says Ingels. "Bakers don't do it, and for that matter, all pastry chefs don't do it equally well. Those who do must do it very well, or not at all."

It is no coincidence that Jean Pierre Piallier, the current chef patissier, makes a parallel statement. While the main function of the hotel's pastry kitchen is to supply all forms of bread, pastries, baked desserts, cakes, petits fours, cookies, ice-cream and sherbet, the decorative pieces make up an important part of elegant presentation.

When the Adolphus celebrated its reopening in 1981, Piallier made an exact replica of the whole Adolphus block in

Jean Pierre Piallier's pastry model of the hotel was one of the marvels at the hotel's reopening in 1981.

a gum paste called pastillage. In addition to 150 hours of his expertise, the model required 250 pounds of powdered sugar, 12 pounds of gelatine and four gallons of egg whites.

A special attraction in the lobby at Christmas time, made by Piallier, required more than 300 man hours and 500 pounds of sugar to 50 pounds of gelatine, but the 6' x 9' mountain village was spectacular. It featured a colorfully decorated church with stained-sugar windows, electrically lighted houses, Santa

Claus, rabbits, children and the Adolphus Train of Restaurants.

From a vat of caramelized sugar, Jean Pierre sculpts bright satin-finish roses to fill a basket woven from the same pulled sugar. Even simple sugar boxes receive chocolate "A" monograms in Piallier's kitchen, and chocolate-coated truffle sleighs are adorned with crystallized violets and roses.

"A good pastry chef must be an artist in the medium of sugar and must be willing to create anything upon request," says Piallier. To that end, a sign on the pastry kitchen wall declares: "*NO PROBLEM* is the name of the pastry kitchen." But, he makes it sound easy: "We make only the small recipe of puff pastry, sometimes," he says, "for 250 pounds, rather than the full 500." Or simple garden baskets made of almonds and sugar. Or bread in the shape of fish, birds and alligators. No Problem.

*   *   *

Despite the Grande Dame's serious facade, funny and unpredictable things have happened there on a regular basis. Beginning in the early Twenties, the staff could count on a Friday laugh when the 57-member (out of respect for Heinz Varieties) Bonehead Club moved its weekly luncheons from the Oriental to the Adolphus. Actually composed of a prestigious, seriously involved group of men, the club became famous for a seriously non-serious approach to life. The Adolphus provided a dramatic backdrop for many non-historical events as the 57 Vice-Presidents planned the 57th ground floor of their 56-story non-building, held their May 3 Christmas party, honored their Bonehead of the Year Award winner, and, on behalf of a mythical Bonehead University, graciously declined to play in the Rose Bowl each year.

"On our annual Look-Up Day, the fun started outside the hotel on the corner of Commerce and Akard," says former Big Chief and Historian Bradford J. Angers. "The first Bonehead to get there started looking upward; when the second arrived, they started to point up to the building and speculate in whispers. More and more came; then we all went inside to lunch. When we came out, there could be a mob, police, firemen . . . all staring skyward."

Stars of the magnitude of Bob Hope were left literally speechless when they were invited to the Adolphus to address the Boneheads. When Hope got up to speak, all the members rose from their chairs and left. They would do the same to

John Wayne. Nevertheless, some very serious matters were resolved there, according to Brad Angers.

One meeting during the Fifties concerned the plight of a broken-hearted giraffe at the Dallas Zoo. It seems that he was dying on the vine with no prospects of a spouse in sight. A Bonehead grant dispatched Clyde Beaty (well-known in circus circles) to Nairobi to scout a sexy giraffe with long, slim legs, a graceful, curved throat, and thick black eyelashes. When the bride arrived, a long white veil was ordered; Haggar, no less, made the groom's trousers. Judge Dick Dixon was asked to witness the exchange of ceremonial rings. The happy couple intertwined their necks for the kiss. "From that union," concludes Angers, "the first USA-native giraffe was born in captivity."

The Boneheads are sentimental about the Adolphus. When the hotel was closed for remodeling in 1980, they celebrated its cornerstone; when the doors were re-opened, the Boneheads came to take up the carpeting. An era either began or ended, whichever it was.

* * *

Century Room Entertainment in the 30's

During the Thirties, while many people still had plenty of money for entertainment, too many others had to save up for special occasions. Those occasions were best served at the Adolphus, where big name bands were constantly booked into the ballroom, or later, in the Century Room for dancing.

"They all came," says Frank Harting, who handled the hotel's public relations at the time, "Tommy and Jimmy Dorsey, Harry James, Benny Goodman, even Leon Belasco and the Andrews Sisters."

Harting booked all the acts, including Phil Harris and Leah Ray for the grand opening of the Century Room. "The Century Room really caught on," he says. "It had a national reputation for good entertainment in the big band era, and was sold out every night." After a long, exciting career in public relations and journalism, Harting still prizes his picture of Phil and Leah. "They came back every year," he recalls. In the thirty years of Century Room entertainment following their opening, all kinds of entertainers came there. The Adolphus housed several good orchestras as well: Ligon Smith, Herman Waldman, and Joe Reichman.

The Adolphus Coffee Shop, managed by "Miss Marie," was the most popular place in town for lunch in 1934. Fifty years later, here's something most people never knew: "When the vote came up in 1934 for liquor by the drink," Harting says,

*Phil Harris and
Leah Ray were good
friends and great
talent at the
Adolphus.*

"we all assumed it would be voted in overnight and we
wanted to present the first bar. So that night we hastily gutted
the coffee shop, stocked it with bar glasses and counters, and
fitted it out for a cocktail lounge. When the vote failed to pass,
we scrambled it back to a coffee shop in time for business as
usual."

The Centennial of 1936 brought many celebrities to Dallas.
Even the Roosevelts came. The President reportedly used back
elevators, in order to hide the great effort it cost him to walk.
Another time, Amelia Earhart stayed at the hotel. "It was the
best place," says Harting, admittedly with some bias; then,
remembering a phrase he coined long ago, he adds, "A bird in
the Busch was worth two in the Baker."

"Fuller Stevens was the manager of the hotel in the '30s. He
had come down from Cincinnati to work with Ralph Hitz," according to his widow, Mina Stevens Lindsley. "They had
worked together in the hotel business for years," she says,

"and had promoted the hotel together going around the country in a two-seater plane." It was an exciting time at the Adolphus, and "Steve" knew how to make the most of it.

If any single portion of Adolphus history brings forth a sigh of, "Ah, those were the days," it is the Century Room era, from 1936 until 1965. And to go a step further, if the Century Room's smashing success could be ascribed to entertainers in the order of the length of their engagements, Dorothy Franey and her Ice Revue skate away with the credit. The timing was

Dorothy Franey, "Queen of the Ice Show," and other stars of the revue. The ice show was a perennial favorite.

perfect for Dorothy Franey's ice show presentations in the Century Room. Most Southwest citizens had never seen skating on ice, except for a few Sonja Henie movies, and her fourteen-year engagement introduced that unfamiliar artform to Dallas. Many a birthday, graduation or bridal fete began at noon when the retractable dance floor rolled back under the stage, revealing an ice floor below.

Show-owner/producer Franey and her troupe made easy work of twirling like tops, or leaping high in their brief, fur-trimmed or glittery costumes. It was only when some non-skater took an ill-advised step onto the ice floor that it became obvious that simply remaining vertical in flat shoes could be tricky. "Fortunately," says the star, "we never had any injuries. More people went through there than Grand Central Station; it was always fun!"

The Century Room was fun, all agree, but it was strenuous work for the entertainers, with a noon show and two at night. Behind the glitter, the skaters had to be serious athletes. Before Dorothy Franey brought her act to the Century Room, she had made a name for herself in speed skating with two Olympic teams, holding eleven out of a possible fourteen world speed skating records. While her shows were running in several cities, Miss Franey also excelled in golf, swimming, diving and track. She hasn't given up sports yet. In 1983, she was elected president of the U.S. Olympians.

At Noon, the skaters performed before an audience quite different from the dining-dancing evening set. The Century Room was filled with debs, housewives, children's birthday parties, bridal fetes, graduation luncheons, market participants and hotel guests. The Noon ice show also brought fans from points outside of, but within driving distance of, Dallas.

Mrs. Eugene Bragg Smith, Sr., for instance, especially remembers the eight winters she spent in Quanah, Texas, when she drove to Dallas regularly to shop and have lunch at the Century Room. "Cotton is a seasonal business," she says, "and we moved back and forth between Montgomery, Alabama, and Quanah, spending some time at the Adolphus on the way." Once they got to Quanah, the excitement of the hotel dining room, filled with interesting people ("I met Sheppard King there," she recalls), the pleasure of professional entertainment, and the sheer beauty of the decor and paintings kept drawing her back. But "shopping" was the reason she gave her mother-in-law. Mrs. Smith laughs to remember,

"One day she said to me, 'Mary, you shop like the rattlesnakes were after you!'"

"Shopping did provide a valid reason to come have lunch in Dallas," says Alice Warren. "Mother and I drove down from Ada, Oklahoma, every chance we had. It was THE thing to do," she says, "to have a whole day of shopping at Neiman-Marcus, with lunch at the Century Room."

If Alice thought the Adolphus was fun in her schooldays, she found it even more exciting in 1958 . . . you never knew whom you might meet there. "It was just after the first

Right: Mrs. H. K. Wasoff and Mrs. J. M. Haggar entertain 7th grade Ursuline graduates. Below: Debs and escorts were astonished by Patsy Gannon's flower display. Below right: Bob Wollebak and 1945 Woodrow Wilson graduates.

Neiman-Marcus Italian Fortnight; I was a buyer in Children's Apparel at the time," she says. "Stanley Marcus, Renee Mazza (a portrait artist) and Leon Harris, of A. Harris and Co., were all being honored with the Italian Award of Solidarity. And these two fascinating Italian men were there . . ." Later that year, the same fascinating Italian men wined and dined Alice in Rome and Milan.

* * *

"Some big name bands were relatively unknown when they came to the Ballroom, or the Roof Garden on the 15th Floor, or the Palm Garden on the very top," says Ligon Smith, whose band played the Century Room for five of the Ice Revue years. "Artie Shaw and Glenn Miller came, and Carmen Cavallero,

the Dorseys and Harry James," Smith says. "Herman Waldman played there for more than five years, and Joe Reichman's orchestra had a long term engagement. We all seemed to go back and forth between the Adolphus and Baker Hotels, but those were the two liveliest places to be."

Entertainers Ligon Smith, left, and Dale Evans and Herman Waldman, had their own Adolphus stories.

At dinner, the evening show was even more dazzling than the Noon show, and it was followed by an evening of dancing. "Three or four times each week, we broadcast live on KRLD," says Smith. "I still have a tape of the original broadcast. We sometimes came on the radio at Noon, but mostly it was at 11:00 P.M."

Namedroppers and autograph hounds had a field day at the Adolphus in those days; any celebrities staying there or at the Baker visited both the Century Room and the Baker's Mural Room. On some occasions, visitors were asked to perform, and they always were introduced, at least. Dale Evans, for example — a singer before she married Roy Rogers — was asked to sing. After the ice-show, she started to make her way up to the bandstand. "But," says Ligon, "someone neglected to roll back the floor . . ." Unfortunately, it was still icy-side up.

Wartime and USO tours also brought some unexpected but priceless additions of talent to Ligon Smith's Century Room scene. Smith relates: "Fred McMurray and Dick Powell were staying at the Adolphus, along with the rest of a USO group. When they came to the Century Room that evening, they joined my band for about an hour, with McMurray playing the saxophone and Powell on the trumpet." Of course, they brought down the house.

As the Thirties wound down, war clouds had not yet begun to clutter the Dallas horizon. Europe was half a world away. If Europe came up in a conversation at all, especially around the fashionable Hotel Adolphus, the topic was either apparel news or an item in the society section of the newspaper about someone sailing for the Continent. Life itself seemed to offer clear sailing, at the moment, with the Depression years on their way out.

For that matter, to the young beautiful debutante class of 1939, the Depression seemed as far away as Europe. At least, it didn't stand in the way of beautiful debutante balls at the hotel, such as the ball given by the E.J. Gannons for their daughter, Patsy.

"O'Hara Watts escorted me to the ball," says Patsy Gannon Campbell, now of Amarillo, Texas, reminiscing about her debut. "The entire Adolphus ballroom was banked with real greenery and artificial camellias. They weren't even real," she says now, "but it seemed such an elaborate, grand setting at the time." They did look real, apparently. "Tom Slick, who came from Oklahoma for the ball, refused to believe they were artificial," she says. The extravagance of those artificial camellias probably was the talk of Dallas. In 1939, the cost of artificial flowers exceeded by far the expense of real flowers. Now, of course, real flowers cost more than silk ones. Greenhouse flowers were probably limited in availability in 1939, and air delivery wasn't common. People either used expensive artificial flowers in large quantity, or real ones in small lots.

*　　*　　*

In 1940, SMU fraternity brothers and their co-eds were

swinging to big band sounds in the grand ballroom, when such dancing was not allowed on the proper SMU campus. After Pearl Harbor and the beginning of World War II, the scene in the Adolphus changed dramatically. It seemed as though frivolity itself marched off to war, as dancing shoes were abandoned for GI boots.

1941 had been a good year for hotel manager H. Fuller Stevens. He had married a lovely woman, with a Joan Bennett look about her, and they were living in the Penthouse of the Adolphus. "We were sitting in the breakfast area on that December day when the President announced the declaration of war. After that, it seemed as though there were always military people there, mainly after the 8th Service Command came to Hensley Field," Mina Lindsley recalls. "One really big conference took place for 40 high-ranking officers. The Undersecretary of War, Robert Patterson, came, as well as Lt. General Brehon Somervell, the Commanding General of the Army Service Forces. Of course, Major General Richard Donovan, Commanding General of the 8th Service Command, attended." For that occasion, the food had to be prepared on the same floor, so the military would lose no time, but, for whatever festivity that one could find in it, Prosper Ingels carved an ice anti-aircraft gun. The air-conditioned officers club on the mezzanine hosted several hundred commissioned officers at open house.

Music played a definite part in the wartime effort to boost the national morale. "KRLD had begun broadcasting from the Adolphus in 1936," says Elizabeth Peabody, "but the field of radio broadcast reached a new peak during the war years. KRLD was an exciting place to be." The young assistant and copywriter was thrilled to find Bob Hope and "Professor" Jerry Colonna sitting on her desk, one afternoon. They were preparing their self-styled ad-libs and plugging their show.

"Kate Smith made some radio history at KRLD, too," says Elizabeth. The full-figured lady was broadcasting from a tiny, uncomfortable studio, describing a beautiful birthday cake made for her by the chef patissier. In her sweetest voice, she wished all the children listening could be there. Then, thinking the show was over and anxious to escape the studio confines, she added a few more well-chosen words, unaware that the sound system was still open to the listening audience.

When the War Bond Show brought General Mark Clark to the Cotton Bowl for an appearance, and hence to the Adolphus, Mrs. Peabody attended the show and the dance

The Adolphus Enters the War Years

which followed in the Grand Ballroom with the General's aide
. . . a young staff sergeant named Bert Parks, who emceed the
show. She had no idea that this jeep-driving soldier would
eventually become Miss America's leading man.

The Adolphus scene was military, political and serious, but
the times were interesting: House Speaker Sam Rayburn
hosted a dinner there, probably arranged by his sister Fannie
Mae. Mina and Fuller Stevens had moved out onto Strait Lane
with their two small children. "That's where we lived when
the Busch family sent the children a tiny grey Sicilian donkey.
Out there, at that time, we could simply hitch a wagon to it
and let the children ride. They loved it! Later we gave the
donkey to the Variety Club."

Other things were fun to remember: the time, for example,
when the huge, fetlocked Clydesdale horses came to town in
special railroad cars. They came to pull an Anheuser-Busch
wagon in a parade. "They were beautiful," says Mina, "but we
had no idea they were so BIG." But, of course, draft horses
must be much larger and heavier than ordinary riding or car-
riage horses . . . at least 1,600 pounds.

"The Busches were a warm, nice family," says Mina.
However, when they came to their board meeting each year in
February, everyone jumped to attention to satisfy every whim.
Petite Marmite Soup and *Souffle* Potatoes, their favorites, were
on every menu. Two waiters simply stood outside their suites,
just in case they wanted anything. Prosper Ingels remembers
testing their sample of brewer's yeast for them. Their visits
were colorful. A relative of theirs, Otto Schubert, managed the
hotel for a time, after Fuller Stevens resigned to join partners
in ownership of several hotels.

*   *   *

By the time Leo Francis Corrigan came to Dallas in 1915, the
Hotel Adolphus had dominated the skyline for two years.
Coincidentally, Corrigan came from the same city where
Adolphus Busch had built his fortune, St. Louis, Missouri. Cor-
rigan married Clara Redman in 1917; they had two children.

As founder of Corrigan Properties, Inc., a large commercial
real estate development firm, Corrigan's main business interest lay in the acquisition of shopping centers, apartment
and office buildings and hotels. He especially liked collecting
old, traditional hotels, and the Adolphus, which he purchased
from the Busch family in 1949, seems to have been a favorite
among them. Corrigan put a chapel in the hotel. It is said that
he walked over every floor of the hotel each day.

During the time Corrigan owned the Adolphus, Commerce Street at Akard was the scene of big name entertainment, the site of a constant schedule of trade markets and conventions, and the hub of many social events. The Adolphus shared most of the activity with the neighboring Baker Hotel, but since they were the only first-class hotels downtown, there was never cause for more than a wholesome rivalry between them. Gradually, as newer, bigger hotels were built downtown, the Adolphus started to show its age.

Of all his Properties, Leo Corrigan was perhaps proudest of the Adolphus.

After Corrigan's death in 1975, the Adolphus was redecorated in part and eventually sold in 1980. The purchasing group, Westgroup, Inc., and the New England Mutual Life Insurance Company spent $45,000,000 to restore and update the old hotel.

Dallas remembers Corrigan in connection with other business interests: he was a director of the Mercantile National Bank, the First National Bank in Dallas (now called InterFirst), and United Fidelity Life Insurance Company. Corrigan was the first president of the Dallas Central Business District Association.

*   *   *

Everyone seems to have a favorite memory from the Century Room. "Hallie Hunter, Elizabeth Peabody's mother, provided mine," says Mrs. Ben E. Cabell, Jr., remembering the birthday party given by her close friend. "She had Bob Crosby sing a personal 'Happy Birthday' to me," she says, "and a visiting photographer took our picture together." Sifting through memories of a family which produced three generations of mayors, including her mayor pro tem husband, Mrs. Cabell says, "It seems that everything used to happen either on one side of Commerce Street at the Adolphus, or at the Baker Hotel on the other." She's right; for several decades, everything did happen there.

To Mrs. Cabell's talented daughter, Sarah Lee Pavey, perhaps the biggest thrill in the Century Room came about when the Dorothy Franey skaters twirled in costumes Sarah had designed for a Neiman-Marcus event. The arts are Sarah's love, and she remembers exactly which side of Commerce hosted each event. She even remembers what sort of decorations had to be created for it.

The price Sarah pays for talent is having to make decorations for everything. She was always dragging in some kind of oversized thing, such as a seven-by-twelve-foot, stylized, papier-mâché Queen of Hearts. "And 100 matching smaller ones," adds Sarah, "for the opera ball table centerpieces." Once, there were orchids and shadow boxes. Another time, for a symphony ball, hundreds of parasols.

"Occasionally, the decorating became hazardous," she says, thinking of the time, as a young mother-to-be, she had to duck back and press against the wall as cars zoomed up the narrow Adolphus driveway. Also hazardous was the mysterious appearance of a brace of white mice in the hotel elevator, during a ball. By coincidence, a high-school science fair was gathered in the hotel.

"During the War," Sarah says, "The Junior Art League, which sprang from the Dallas Museum of Fine Arts, started entertaining officers with coffee and cookies. When we moved that project to the Adolphus ballroom, it became a regularly scheduled dance for servicemen. That original group banded together to organize the Cotillion Club of Dallas."

Professional groups gathered regularly at the hotel: "Henry," says Juanita Miller, "Why does it seem that we were *always* at the Adolphus?"

"We were, Juanita. The Real Estate Board met there."

"We were there for medical meetings," says Mrs. J.L. Goforth, recalling her husband's involvement in medical organizations. "But sometimes we went to the Century Room for parties." She says, "They had to keep that room so cold, in order to keep the ice floor from melting . . . and, one time, at "Bumps" Henderson's birthday party, she called her mother, Mrs. Legge, to send wraps over for everybody there." Which the lady did!

*　　*　　*

When Randall Davis came to manage the Adolphus in 1947, the hotel was still owned by the Busch family. The Ice Revue was still the hottest cold show in town, and the ballroom was always booked for important dances and big banquets. The Adolphus and the Baker were still the only first-class hotels downtown, so whenever Market rolled around (seemingly fairly often), every room in each hotel was taken.

"There was a different market week for everything," says Randall Davis. "Twice a year: ladies and children's apparel; men's wear; gifts and jewelry; home furnishings; and, trade shows or conventions . . . you name it! We had to stack furniture, or simply take it out of the rooms. Showrooms had to be set up, which, of course, left us with mattresses lining the walls of the corridors." In retrospect, Davis says, "It was a fire hazard by today's standard. Modern fire prevention codes wouldn't have allowed us to do that. And, as though that weren't bad enough, the gift shows made it even worse. All their packing crates and papers had to be stored during the show and then returned to take the samples back to the place of business."

Post-war goods were being imported in 1948, when John and Juliette Daniel opened their gift shop in Lakewood, but the only time to see any of the possible inventory was during Market Week. "Only rarely did the salesmen call on us, and we couldn't go see the goods personally, the way we can now," says Mrs. Daniel. "Although some dealers such as Buchel — milk glass, crystal and gifts — had showrooms in the Merchandise Mart, Rosenthal and Royal Doulton items only appeared at Market, along with the Keepnews Company's fine Dresden pieces. The silver lines were in New York, so we selected the silver at the same time and then had to wait forever to get all of it." The rooms were lined all around up and down, with nothing shown to advantage and crowds of buyers milling through. But, somehow, it was fun: "The highlight was the one big dinner party in the Century Room, with a speaker from one of the big gift or china firms."

Market Week brought Jeanne Eddy to the hotel; she wouldn't have missed it for the world. "When I came to Dallas in the late 40's," she says, "I was looking for a modeling job in the apparel market shows. I asked the reservations manager of the hotel about it, and, after modeling for Junior Sophisticates, I ended up working in sales, catering and public relations with Randall Davis."

But, about markets: "They really did take over the hotels, as well as the Merchandise Mart and the Santa Fe Building," says Jeanne. We had a number of 'sample rooms,' which were set aside for shows and left unfurnished."

Corrigan Properties bought the Adolphus in 1949, and by 1952 they had added a Main Street wing. "They bought the

Business Was Big After the War.

Andrew Building," says Hal Fish, purchasing agent for Corrigan Properties, "which was another Busch-built edifice (though not nearly so grand as the hotel), and built the Adolphus Tower in its place. More and more rooms and wings had become necessary to accommodate Adolphus business, trade shows, markets and conventions. At that point, the number of rooms topped 1,240."

In the middle of the Sixties, when dress manufacturer Herman Marcus was chairman of the board of the American Fashion Association, the apparel market scene was changed significantly. Commercial real estate development in the Industrial area produced a huge market complex built specifically to house the buying and selling exchange of wholesale goods. Marcus, who knew the markets *when*, was impressed.

The fashion markets didn't just happen spontaneously at the hotels on Commerce Street. "We had to build the markets. Way before I had my own company, I remember selling women's dresses on the road," Marcus says. "In 1932, the sales force went out calling on buyers all over the Southwest, but we tried to get them to come in to Dallas on weekends and see all the lines at once."

Travel wasn't as convenient then as it is now. "The roads were so bad," Marcus says. "At best, they were two-lane country roads." With a shake of his head, he adds, "I'll never forget that muddy road between Amarillo and Lubbock, and how we dreaded the idea of car trouble." But if the salesmen made it to Pampa, the Scarborough was their hotel, and, he says, "We sat

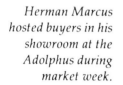

Herman Marcus hosted buyers in his showroom at the Adolphus during market week.

family style at a big table and helped ourselves to whatever was there."

No one seems to sigh for those good old days. "When buyers did start coming to Dallas, staying at the two hotels on Commerce Street, even the hot unairconditioned rooms were a big improvement," says Marcus. "It wasn't really comfortable, but it was better, and we had entertainment."

In the early years of the market system, clothes manufacturers found good sample rooms for $8 per day at the Adolphus Hotel. Herman Marcus used to ask for corner suite

Converted suites made colorless but functional showrooms during markets.

#1462 because it had more room than most. Despite the extra bit of room, however, the hotel staff had to bring in a mattress for the floor at night and take it away in the morning. There was no room for anything but samples.

"By 1939, it was a big deal to come to Dallas to market." says Marcus. "Then, during World War II, the buyers all had to come to market because the gasoline shortage curtailed the traveling sales activity." Also, a shortage of other goods and fabrics had upset the balance of supply and demand. "Instead of pressing sales," says Marcus, "we had to limit the allotment to each customer. They became competitive about the amount they could purchase, bringing gifts such as hard-to-get bottles of Scotch Whiskey."

The rapid growth of the Dallas Market spawned many successful careers. Kim Dawson always believed that enjoying what you do makes hard work worthwhile. "But timing and luck were very important," she says. The market was about to outgrow the Adolphus-Baker location when Kim decided to open her own modeling agency. Also in her favor, Dallas had grown considerably as a clothing manufacturing center.

In the 1950's Kim Dawson modeled exclusively for Neiman-Marcus, showing high fashion weekly in the Mural Room show at the Baker. Zane Hayes, a freelance model, did the A. Harris show in the Century Room. During Market Week, the official breakfast/fashion show opening brought the two friends onto the runway of the same show, with Evelyn Lambert doing the commentary. Both girls had the wholesome, happy kind of beauty associated with Littletown, America, combined with the right amount of pizzazz.

"When I first came to Dallas," says Kim, "all those big buildings and the Flying Red Horse on the Magnolia Building almost overwhelmed me. My home town, Center, Texas, was built around a square. I wanted to build a future here, but first I went to Washington and New York." After meeting Harry Conover, she modeled in New York and then went to Europe to model for Jacques Fath, Jacques Heim and Marcel Rochas. Then she came back to Dallas to Neiman-Marcus.

Zane grew up in Corsicana, with her eye already fixed on a career in Dallas. Driving into the city, she liked to see the Dallas landmark, the Red Horse, turning alongside her other favorite feature, the green-topped Adolphus. Her career materialized right there, at Commerce and Akard.

"Wednesday was the big day for A. Harris models," Zane says, "when Leon Harris brought the weekly fashion show to the Century Room. We didn't even mind that our only place to change clothes was a tiny hallway. The Century Room was good to us starving models, too, treating us to shrimp cocktail, prime rib and strawberry pie."

On the Sunday night before market week started, Ike Clark used to invite the buyers to a Sunday evening fashion show, dinner and dancing in the Century Room. "At one of those, I wore the Clark dress which won the Ruth Fair Alice Dallas Award," says Zane. "Clark was one of the favorites."

"Neiman-Marcus models showed exclusively for the store, in those days," says Kim Dawson, "and I did that. However, once Evelyn Lambert made me be a Christmas tree, wearing a leotard with a tall, green tree headpiece." It was an exception for Kim to model at the Adolphus. However, says Kim, "When Evelyn decided to retire from doing the American Fashion Association show, she suggested that I do it. So I changed the system somewhat by going over to the Adolphus and around the Baker, selecting things I considered the best from each line. I put them together to be a show of the best of the entire market." When Kim decided to open her own agency, her

Kim Dawson and Zane Hayes first established their modeling careers at the Dallas markets.

friend Zane was one of the first models to be listed. Now Kim has the biggest agency in Dallas.

The Adolphus welcomed Kim back in 1981, when she did a style show for the reopening of the hotel. "That show was for the new owners, Westgroup, Inc., and New England Mutual Life Insurance Company, and the Amfac managers," says Kim. "We did *Hello, Texas,* featuring some Texas designers, such as Victor Costa and Mary Lide Murchison. Some furs were shown, and surprises, such as bathing suits worn beneath them."

* * *

One of the favorite days for Randall Davis and Jeanne Eddy came in the early 50's, when General Douglas MacArthur came to Dallas. "He had been relieved of his command by President Harry Truman, but Dallas could hardly wait to see him," says Davis. "He came as a hero," says Jeanne, "and we gave him the ticker tape parade for a hero's welcome. In fact, he was mobbed by people wanting to talk to him, or touch him, or simply to see him. We were really pressed to get him away from the crowd to the safety of the penthouse with Mrs. MacArthur, and his son. My wife Evelyn made cookies for his son, and we had to tear over to A. Harris to find a cookie jar to take up to the Skyway Suite."

Jeanne Eddy's least favorite incident happened during a JAYCEE convention during the worst heat wave of the worst summer in Dallas, when the electrical power failed. "We got the lights back on," she says, "but not the air-conditioning, and there was no elevator service. We had to walk up more than twenty floors to meetings several times each day."

A Center for Nightlife and Talent

Private clubs were not very common in Downtown Dallas in the late 40s and early 50s, but those in existence offered amenities lacking in restaurants. Of these, the Variety Club was one of the smartest places to be seen. The slot machines rolled, rang and rattled half the night.

"The first night I came to Dallas from Long Island, I couldn't imagine what was going on in my closet," says stage designer, Peter Wolf. "The slot machines were just on the other side of it, in the Variety Club. Finally, I decided to see whether I could get in. It was wonderful," he says. "They not only let me in, but also they were willing to take a Manhattan check, which I'm not sure I could have cashed in New York!"

More than thirty years later, Peter Wolf Concepts would be responsible for the restoration of the Adolphus Hotel's grand ballroom, the foyer, and the French Room, all to a point beyond their original elegance.

John Rowley of United Artists explains the Variety Club's *raison d'etre:* "At the time when the Variety Club was in the Adolphus, it was legal for private clubs to have a liquor license, and they also had slot machines. Variety had one of the few decent bars downtown. The amazing phenomenon, however, is that those eight slot machines brought in $150,000 per year for charity."

William O'Donnell, a former president of Variety, explains that the club was actually a charitable institution involved in fundraising for children. "It was organized by and for entertainers and others in the field of amusements, but between 1935 and the mid-50s it was noted as a social club of sorts, patronized by both local and transient guests . . . anyone, in fact, connected with theater, radio and filmmaking."

Jack Bryant managed the Variety Club from 1945 to 1958. "The gambling law wasn't enforced in private clubs at the time they had the machines," he says. "Certainly it wasn't enforced in our case, with the revenue going to charity." When the time of enforcement came, the machines had to go, but the mountings had been set in concrete. Rather than tear up the whole club with a jackhammer, the Adolphus sentenced the one-armed bandits to be covered by a false wall.

The liveliest time for the Variety Club could be defined as the time before television became a common form of entertainment. All show people belonged to the club, so every performer who came to Dallas came up there to relax. Some even performed there, but with 1,400 members and 140 associates, and hours from 11:00 A.M. until 1:00 the following A.M., the club was a beehive, whether there was entertainment or not.

On New Year's Eve, the grand ballroom belonged to the Variety Club Cotton Bowl Association. The coaches and officials of the Cotton Bowl teams were honored at a dinner dance, with a midnight broadcast on KRLD. When SMU won twice, it was especially festive — for everyone except the team. Even team star Doak Walker had to observe strict training rules and retire about 9:00, the hour when the party started.

One of the Century Room favorite sons was Herman Waldman. He had begun playing at the Adolphus on an occasional basis in the late Twenties or early Thirties. "We all played the Baker and the Adolphus when we were in Dallas," he says. "That's all there was, but Ligon Smith, Joe Reichman and I all had times that we played there for 5-year, or longer, engagements. I played in the Century Room from 1948 to 1956, when I decided to go into the field of investments."

Waldman not only played for the Ice Revue, but he was also there when Manager Randall Davis started a new kind of entertainment in the Century Room. "A big theatrical agency

Hildegarde's appearance at the Century Room turned into a long-run spectacular.

called me in 1951," says Davis. "Singer Hildegarde happened to have a free week on her way to Shreveport, and for a $3 cover charge (all hers), she would sing."

Davis said okay. "Dorothy needed to give up the ice show for about a week at that time, and we didn't have a cover charge anyway, so we had nothing to lose. If people wanted to pay, they could come hear her; if not, the *chanteuse* would simply make less." So Davis went to meet her with an armful of roses, dethorned at Hildegarde's secretary's request.

The lady was a smashing success. On her second day there, Davis worked out a deal with the man in Shreveport to extend

Hildegarde's Century Room appearance. "She drew a capacity crowd and made about $10,000 at $3 per person." As it turned out, Davis had instigated a round of one-upmanship with the Baker. He knew he had a winner when Fenton Baker hurried out to California and booked Sophie Tucker for the Mural Room.

A long parade of special entertainers came through the Century Room after Hildegarde, such as Lauritz Melchior, Tony

Rudy Vallee, Ted Lewis, and Joe Reichman; Reichman with Liberace; and "The Toast of the Town" host Ed Sullivan.

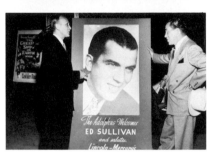

Bennett, Yma Sumac (of the seven-octave voice range), Tony Martin, Mimi Benzell, Evelyn Knight, and the *piece de resistance*, Edith Piaf.

It was a red-letter, black-tie night for Francophiles when Edith Piaf, "The Sparrow of Paris," took the Century Room by storm. Entertainment Critic Tony Zoppi of *The Dallas Morning News* put it this way:

"Not since that saucy 'Madamoiselle from Armentières' stole the affections of the Rainbow Division has a Frenchwoman captured the hearts of Americans as completely as Miss Piaf did Friday night at the Hotel Adolphus Century Room. The tiny Parisian with husky pipes kept the first-nighters spellbound with a variety of tunes which ranged from a weird story of a successful suicide to 'Black Denim Trousers and Motorcycle Boots'." And, further, "She was introduced by Monsier Robert Vernay, manager of Paris' famed Hotel Maurice, who was a guest of the Adolphus' Randall Davis. M. Vernay described her as France's leading Ambassador of Good Will to the United States." For the occasion, the Vincent Bragale Orchestra put on seven extra musicians and played behind a chiffon curtain to emphasize the haunting mood created by La Piaf.

The December 1956 engagement at the Century Room was a break for those who didn't get to see Edith Piaf on her first visit to Dallas. The year before, she had sung at the Neiman-Marcus International Fashion Awards presentation honoring Grace Kelly.

Bob Brock, Entertainment Critic for *The Dallas Times Herald*, described the Piaf performance in the "filled-to-overflowing Adolphus Hotel Century Room," saying "Edith Piaf deserves an adjective all to herself. An adjective to have and to hold, never to be used in reference to any other entertainer . . ." He, like Zoppi, was spellbound: "Miss Piaf is 40-ish, four feet, six inches tall, and never appears on a club floor gowned in anything but a simple black dress. Her short red hair is in disarray, her porcelain-like face has two black strokes over the eyes for brows and a red circle for lips. Yet, this is one of the most expressive faces we have ever seen."

Edith Piaf Wows Audiences at the Adolphus.

Singing in a strong, gutteral voice, with only a wine glass and a towel for props, she simply threw her head back and sang. "If the Century Room had been Paris' Lido, the reception could not have been wilder," Brock concluded. "There are many acts to be seen these days in supper clubs. But there are very few experiences like Edith Piaf."

Reviewing the Century Room era, Brock recalls that Joe E. Lewis came at least once a year. He was one of Brock's favorites. "But his act went beyond the Century Room, and brought a different crowd. He didn't stop when the show was over . . . he simply picked up his drink and continued across the street at the University Club, with another comedian named Ukie Sherin."

Kay Thompson came to the Century Room. "She had a terribly chic act," says Brock, "and she worked Andy and the other Williams Brothers into it. Kay was one of the most sophisticated comediennes. She danced and sang, and, if you recall, she was a writer. Remember *Eloise?* The book about a little girl who lived at The Plaza in New York?"

Chris Elson probably set some kind of record as club owner at the Adolphus from around 1950, when he opened the Burgundy Room and the Kings Club, until the hotel closed in 1980, to say nothing of the late-nighter Kings Club East on the lobby floor, which opened in 1969.

The Kings Club was known for perfect steaks and chops, and continuous live entertainment. Elson kept his own band, led by Lloyd Hebert, and sought out talent on the rise. He brought in Jerry Van Dyke and Roy Clark, two of his favorites, and also Pat Rolle from Nassau, who reminded people of Nat King Cole. Then, Elson brought the Latin American Vega Brothers, who played "Guantanamera" and that sort of thing on two harps, a bongo and a guitar.

Certainly, the bartender at the Kings tried to please. On the basis of Mrs. Elson's description of a drink in Nassau called the West Indies Yellow Bird, the Kings bartender, refusing to be outdone, created his own version called the East Texas Yellow Bird.

Within the Adolphus, members and guests of the Variety and Kings Clubs may have found oases of relaxation and entertainment, but the Dallas Bar Association headquarters, despite its name, didn't even have a bar. That Bar added a note of sobriety, if not outright solemnity, to the hotel's club activity with weekly legal lectures for members.

Tom Unis of the Strasburger Price law firm remembers the Bar Association's inaugural dinner at the hotel in 1950. "Henry Strasburger was president of the Bar Association when we moved over to the Adolphus. Before that time, we had to meet at the Courthouse, on Saturday, when the courts weren't in session. Granted, the meeting room was small, but when a dignitary such as a Supreme Court Judge came to address the Bar Association, we met in the ballroom. It was an improvement to move over there, in any case."

Unis, a former Dallas City Council member who later served as the president of the non-partisan Citizens Charter Association, recalls other political activity at the hotel: "Until the end of the Fifties, and for some time after that, the important fund drives and major political campaigns were initiated there. Then the victory party usually followed in the same place." Unis adds, "Eric Jonsson's mayoral campaign began there, and John Connally's big gubernatorial race fundraiser was held there in 1962."

* * *

The old football feud between Texas and Oklahoma Universities comes to life every year in October, at the Cotton Bowl, during the State Fair of Texas. For the annual pre-game rally and confrontation, the students have staged their traditional encounter on Commerce Street. In years past, Texas Longhorn fans filled the Baker, and Oklahoma Sooners took over the Adolphus. On the following night, usually, one school celebrated loudly and the other left town quietly.

"Ordinarily, the weekend required only fifteen extra security guards to patrol the halls and break up the usual good-natured fights," says Randall Davis, "although we always made arrangements for the house doctor to stay at the hotel all night."

"But then there was THAT year, 1958," says Jane Peterson, nee Hufendick, of Dallas, "when Texas beat Oklahoma for the first time in ten years. It was my first year at Texas University, and I expected it to be rowdy, just from what I had heard. But it was total chaos! Windows were broken out in some buildings between Akard and St. Paul Streets, and from the hotel windows, airborne furniture landed on the sidewalk of Commerce."

Ann Hufendick Hamman of Houston, Jane's sister, recalls that 1958 chaos, too. Ann was the Sweetheart of The University of Texas that year. "Oh, yes, I remember that it was the worst year," she says. "But since we didn't have rooms in the hotel, we didn't see the worst of it."

Texas/OU Fans Converge Yearly on the Hotel

"The New Year's Cotton Bowl celebration was a little bit more tame," she recalls, "but that was celebrated around the hotels, too, with parties and luncheons. Also, everyone hung off those same balconies to watch on that freezing cold day when we rode in the Cotton Bowl Parade."

The following year, the downtown merchants arranged a dance to try to keep the students off the street. "It wasn't a huge success," says Davis, "but at least the weekend was a lesser nightmare than the year before that."

Occasionally, serious efforts were made to discourage the tide of college students surging up into the hotel and sweeping out onto the balconies. Sometimes, the situation seemed to be hopeless, with the lobby covered with debris and glass. One year, the hotel borrowed the 7-foot doorman, Bill Bass, from La Tunisia Restaurant, gave him a top hat and paid him double shift for his presence at the Commerce Street entrance. Those who didn't have room keys were tapped on top of the head with the suggestion, "Look, why don't you go on to some other place?" He was pleasant but rather startling.

Those days may be over, now that the Adolphus is in a new era and the Baker is long gone. The pre- and post-game street scenes have calmed down quite a lot. The Texas-OU weekend fell just two weeks after the reopening in 1981. The best idea seemed to be to close, other than to hotel guests or those with dining reservations.

"Not that it was quiet . . . there was activity in the street," says Betty Holloway, Director of Public Relations for the Adolphus. Last year, too, while CBS was filming Commerce Street from the garage entrance, there was some confusion, but nothing like it has been in the past. On the inside, it seemed to be a normal weekend. On one side of the hotel, the Texas Legislature was meeting at dinner, while, on the other side, King Olaf of Norway was hosting his Annual Leiv Eriksson Banquet."

* * *

By 1957, Randall Davis was no longer at the hotel, and a whole different phase began with H.H. "Andy" Anderson at the manager's desk. Other major hotels, the Statler Hilton and the Sheraton, had already come to Dallas. For the automobile-minded, outlying motels had started to replace the traditional hotel accommodations. For the first time, the hotel needed some promotion to make people sit up and take notice. Anderson called in Stormy Meadows to create some public interest in the hotel, a departure from her show-biz promotional experience. Well, maybe it wasn't such a departure, with show people around the hotel so frequently . . . and more of them came: Irving Berlin, Talullah Bankhead, Bing Crosby, Edgar Bergen, Liberace, even Rudy Vallee.

Stormy knew how to get attention. Rather than send a limousine to meet Gene Autry at Love Field, Stormy put on the western regalia she usually reserved for cowboy star Chill Wills, and went to meet Autry herself. Pulling up to the gate in a wagon driven by a team of mules, Stormy presented a horsecollar to the western star.

"But that wasn't the living end," says Stormy, "The living end came when I rented a hearse and went to meet the president of the National Tire Dealers." Accompanied by a bellman in tails and a cocktail waitress in a long dress, carrying a bucket of dry ice, Stormy offered that man a drink instead of a horsecollar. She then drove him to the hotel in the hearse. "He nearly died."

Anderson left some other colorful arrangements to Stormy. "One Texas-OU weekend," she says, "a sheriff and his marshal from Lubbock came and insisted on a room. Every broom closet was full, but Andy told me to move twin beds into the hotel chapel. The men slept there, alright," she says, "but they thought it would be too irreverent to drink there, so they set up their bar at the door and drank out in the hall."

* * *

Although the hotel presented popular music, fun, and entertainment in the Century Room, the Adolphus had a highbrow side, too. Each time the Metropolitan Opera brought its magic to the State Fair Music Hall, the singers gathered in the Adolphus to attend the formal ball following the opera performance. And when local patrons decided to put together a Dallas Civic Opera, the organization first took root at the hotel, where the Leo Corrigans and the Henry Millers could keep a watchful eye on it.

"It was because of Leo that the Dallas Civic Opera was connected with the hotel," says Juanita Miller. "Leo enjoyed supporting the opera, and so did we. So, we had the first opera ball in the grand ballroom. The year we organized the Dallas Civic Opera, Maria Callas came to sing a benefit concert." In a moment of triumph for the DCO, the Millers rode to the airport in a city car with Mayor R.L. Thornton and the opera director, Larry Kelly, to meet Maria Callas and take her to the hotel. At the concert, Miss Callas performed the letter scene from *MacBeth* and sang double arias from *La Traviata* and *I Puritani*.

Maria Callas made opera-lovers out of everyone, including host Henry Miller, at right.

"She was wonderful," recalls Juanita Miller, "the consummate, most thorough artist, despite her turbulent personal life." Callas returned to sing *La Traviata* in full in 1958, and *Medea*. In 1959, she came again, to sing *Lucia di Lammermoor* and *The Barber of Seville*.

* * *

The late Andy Anderson already knew quite a lot about the Adolphus when he replaced Randall Davis as Managing Director in 1957. Beginning as a 13-year-old bellhop thirty years before, Andy had worked at the hotel in several different capacities. He had an engaging smile, and he was willing to take on anything. From time to time, he moved on to bigger and better things, but he always came back. Young Andy loved the hotel, and the Grande Dame was always glad to welcome his return, especially if the youth had been dismissed for some trivial oversight, such as leaving a grand piano on the roof during a rainstorm.

When Andy moved into the hotel in 1957, he brought his wife, Dotty, and their two children, David and Ann. He decided that kids need a back yard, and proceeded to put an eight-foot fence around the flat part of the rooftop. He had it

The rooftop "playground in the sky" was a special place for managers' kids in the 50's.

landscaped and planted with roses, pansies, and jonquils. Then he added swings, a slide, and a small wading pool for the children. Everyone called it "that great playground in the sky."

"I was the hotel's 'Eloise, except without the water in the mail chute," says Ann Holmes, the Andersons' daughter. "That playground was built for my brother David and me. That's where we played, had our annual Easter egg hunt, and buried our dead hamsters in the rosebushes. From 1957 through 1965, we lived on the top floor, with the playground just down the hall."

Ann and David thought the natural way of life for all children included room service and feasts of lobster and prime rib, and even a chauffeur to drive them to school. Moreover, they believed that all birthday parties were catered by Prosper Ingels, the *chef patissier*. Hotel balconies offered box seats for passing parades (the picture of the Kennedy parade was taken from one of them). "It was fun," says Ann. "The PBX staff gave me my own head set: Florence Miller, who had a cosmetics shop down in the arcade, taught me how to blend face powder." Yet, the only place to try out a new Christmas bike or skates was the hotel corridor, and only a deserted lobby allowed the furtive toss of a football. Cartwheels had to be quick!

Nothing about the grandeur of the Adolphus intimidated Dotty. She had grown up in a house in St. Louis that was originally built for Busch's family. The traditional elegance of the hotel seemed familiar, somehow, and Dotty appreciated it. She could see signs of the hotel's having seen better days. Interested in interior design, she did some redecorating of rooms. She especially liked the old chandelier with the eagles and hops. "That fixture never needed polishing," she says. "It might have gold plate on it." Leo Corrigan liked it, too. "He insisted on keeping it where it was when he bought the hotel," she adds. "After all, it was attached." Only a few Busch family artifacts remain in the hotel. The family took their paintings, except for the one (now on loan) which shows hunting dogs and pheasants, hanging in the entrance to the Grille Restaurant of the Adolphus. In Corrigan's day, his own collection of European paintings hung from the paneled lobby walls.

Nothing ever really surprised Andy Anderson; he had been in the hotel business a long time. When President Harry

Harry Truman and Ronald Reagan each made visits to the hotel: one a president; one a president to be.

Truman came to Dallas, Andy gave him the VIP treatment, sending up a basket of fruit, a bottle of Scotch, and a bottle of Bourbon whiskey. A few minutes later the phone rang. "Andy?" said Give-'Em-Hell Harry, "thanks a lot for the bottles. Could I trade the Scotch for another bottle of Bourbon instead?"

* * *

A Quiet Social Statement in Changing Times

During the Fifties, some quiet, dignified social statements were made in the Grande Dame's parlor. Even before the movies told us to "Guess Who Is Coming ..." Willie Mays came to dinner with the Cleveland Indians and New York Giants.

Juanita Craft, former Dallas City Councilwoman, tells a nice story about the Adolphus. She saw the beginning transition to desegregation. Actually, Juanita Craft effected two separate changes in Adolphus policy, one during the Fifties but another way back in the Twenties. Flash back to 1925, when Juanita joined the staff of the hotel to become the first woman in their bell service — or, as Foster Prather put it, "the first bellperson."

"It was the first time a woman did that kind of work," she says. "I took small bags up for the ladies, and brought them ginger ale with ice; or, I helped them unpack and, if a dress needed to be pressed, I took care of it for the lady. I did get to meet some interesting people." To name one, Charles Lindberg, in 1927. "Ladies came from everywhere and brought their daughters to meet him," she says. "In fact, they offered me a lot of money, if I would help them get closer to where he was."

Juanita left the hotel in 1934. The early Depression Years hurt the hotel trade, just as they did every kind of business. It became difficult to make more than daily carfare for transportation to and from the Adolphus. She hated to leave; Juanita had been in the bell service for nine years.

The Fifties directed Juanita back to the Adolphus to achieve another quiet first for equal rights. As chairman of the reception committee for the Americans for Democratic Action, she was welcomed in the front door of the hotel, escorting her champion, Eleanor Roosevelt, to the Presidential Suite. "They were glad to see me," Juanita recalls. "I'd had good experience in the hotel. They knew I could take the lady right to her suite."

* * *

Something about the Adolphus seemed to draw St. Louis people, and bandleader Joe Reichman felt right at home. Joe had been playing in and out of the hotel for years, just as Ligon Smith and Herman Waldman did. They all had turns playing for deb parties and the social club dances in both of the big Commerce Street hotels. Then, in the late Fifties, Joe made his home in a suite at the Adolphus and directed the house orchestra until the middle of the Sixties, when the Century Room was closed. Joe had a way of making everyone feel welcome.

"The Adolphus had a national reputation as the center of entertainment, and the Century Room had incredible appeal," says Johnny Desmond, who sang his first, two-week Dallas engagement there with Joe Reichman in the late Fifties.

Desmond's booking there was inevitable. "Every entertainer who was anyone had played there, including two of my own big band leaders: Glenn Miller and Bob Crosby," he says, "But I missed it both times. My career didn't really get underway until Glenn requisitioned me to sing with the Air Force Band he put together during World War II."

Desmond calls the Century Room a good luck charm which brought him back many times to play in Dallas. More than that, really . . . he happened to make a down payment on a little farm just north of Dallas with his Century Room earnings, now worth about forty-five times the gamble. No wonder Desmond is a Texan convert.

Canadian-Dallasite Louise Buckspan remembers the Century Room era well. The entertainers were first class, yet the Century Room itself seemed small and personal. The Buckspans liked to go there on a fairly regular basis.

"Joe Reichman made it seem like a private club," Louise says. "He called everybody by name, and played whatever kind of music we were in the mood to hear." She recalls that the Adolphus still played an important part during Market Week. "My Lady Buxton showroom was at the old Merchandise Mart," she says, "but the two hotels had rooms for temporary shows. Before we had the Trammell Crow complex of markets and trade centers, those three places, along with the old Santa Fe Building, made up the entire showroom area for wholesale markets." After hours, the market-weary met in the Century Room to relax. A new song and dance review called "Bottoms Up" was playing.

Ann Reichman Norvell remembers, "Big name acts and live entertainment had made the Century Room the premier supper club. New things started there. I came to the Adolphus when Breck Wall and Joe Peterson put together a new kind of show. They found me on campus at TCU, in Fort Worth."

Big name entertainment had become too expensive, but Joe Reichman knew that new talent could be a welcome change. He worked with Breck and Joe to get the original "Bottoms Up" show going in the hotel. Two stand-up comics named Rowan and Martin, who were playing at the Statler-Hilton, came down to watch it, eventually, and bought the format for their own "Laugh-In" television show.

"It was a different kind of thing for the Century Room," says Breck Wall, "or for any place. It was all new, with ten people who sang, danced, and did topical humor. The first show was booked for a two-week run, with a two week option," he says, "but it was a real hit. It ran non-stop for two years before closing."

Century Room revues set a fast pace and launched careers for young Dallas talent.

Later, Wall and Peterson did other shows, such as RAZZ-MA-TAZZ. That one boosted KVIL's Suzie Humphreys into a career in Dallas radio and television, just shortly after she

came to Dallas from San Antonio. By day, she was Suzanne Malone, working in public relations at Texas Bank and Trust Co.; at night, she became "Bertha DeBlues." "And, in between," Suzie says, "we gathered in Breck's room to sew sequins on our costumes. Finally, it was easier just to move into the Adolphus, to economize on both time and money. We really poor-boyed that show!

"The room I had on the 7th floor was right where the addition rooftops came together. All I could see was the rooftops and a few pigeons." But, if you think the view from the window was bad, she says, "At the entrance to my room, there was a line of chairs down the hall. It looked pretty strange, unless you knew that the Southwest Shoes Association was located on seven, too." Shoe Salesmen's Row, it was called.

"Bottoms Up" also introduced the beautiful Sutton sisters to their hometown audience. Kay won a screen test, and went to New York to do fashion modeling. Jan stayed with the show.

Ann Reichman had played in several shows before she and Joe were married. "Joe was a good-hearted man," she says. "He wanted everyone to have a good time. His motto was 'Music for Dancing,' and he did all but light a fire under people. He could hardly stand to see people not dance, so he would find out what the crowd wanted to hear and would play that kind of music."

The secret of Joe Reichman's music lay in keeping it young. He moved forward with changing beats, instead of hanging on to the past. When the Twist first squirmed its way into the Century Room, Joe went out and found instructor-couples to demonstrate. The crowd was delighted to discover that they could actually move that way. Still, if they wanted to waltz, Joe played waltzes.

Ann modeled shoes for Jim Verdon at shoe market. "Wing Dings," she says. "Up until that time, tennis shoes were simply made for athletic wear. These were plaids or mattress ticking stripes, really innovative designs." They were advertised once by a live pink horse on Commerce Street, to call attention to the fact that their showroom had a "horse of a different color." Ann's favorite horse, however, was the three-story Pegasus high atop the Magnolia Building. "My small son and I used to watch it at close range from 'that great playground in the sky.' "

The Grande Dame saw some embarrassing moments in 1960, when then-Senator Lyndon B. Johnson came to Dallas to try to win Texas over to the Kennedy-LBJ ticket. A rabble, generally associated with support groups for Senator Bruce Alger, was in the rousing at the Baker when LBJ and Ladybird arrived. It had gotten out of hand by the time he made his way over to the Adolphus for a luncheon. The group had become a full-blown mob scene, complete with nasty signs accusing Johnson of "selling out to Yankee Socialists." Somebody snatched Ladybird's gloves and threw them into the gutter; somebody else spit. It was a tense, anxious half hour.

In the lobby of the Adolphus, the senator stood tall, held his lady close by and made the most of the moment, politically, with the benefit of television, radio and press coverage. He said, "If the time has come when I can't walk through the lobby of a hotel in Dallas with my lady without a police escort, I want to know it." Actually, the time hadn't come yet, but it would come within a couple of years. When it did, he was among the first to know. In November of 1963, he no doubt remembered saying those words in the hotel lobby.

* * *

The flier said: "A DAY TO REMEMBER — JUNE 17, 1908: A DAY TO CELEBRATE: JUNE 17, 1983." The Dallas Advertising League came home to the Adolphus to celebrate the 75th Anniversary of their founding.

A Day They Won't Forget

"The Ad League is the oldest civic luncheon club in Dallas," says advertising consultant Jerry Burford. "From it came the Better Business Bureau, the Salesmanship Club, Civitan and the Rotary Club. The League brought Dallas its first convention of 5,000 people in 1912, shortly after the Adolphus was opened. As early as 1929, the Ad League put on forerunners to the Press Club of Dallas Gridiron Shows. Burford remembers when they established the Advertising Club of Dallas at the Adolphus.

The Advertising Club was private, for League members and graphic arts people. For Jerry, who was a Vice-President and Director of Marketing for Dallas Federal Savings and Loan at the time, going to lunch at the club was the way to do three days business in one hour. By 1960, the Advertising Club had moved into the Variety Club quarters on the 7th floor. The now-famous slot machines had disappeared. "But everyone knew where they were," says Gale Sliger, who managed the club for 13 years. It was only a matter of time before holes would be cut into the false wall during a renovation. Those now-famous slot machines were hauled away to become decorative props.

The Advertising Club really catered to a different group from the Variety, but old members of Variety still drifted in unheralded. It wasn't unusual to find someone like Georgie Jessell dispensing stories from his barstool.

One of the city's most dramatic events left the Advertising League stricken. Gale Sliger was there on November 22, 1963, while the Ad League's Board of Directors held a meeting.

"Mike Shapiro, Manager of Channel 8, was there," she says, "and Jim Lovell of *The Dallas Times Herald*, and other press/radio/tv leaders." Gale had left them to their meeting while she joined a happy, excited crowd on the Main Street side of the hotel to see President John F. Kennedy and lovely,

The passing of the Kennedy entourage and its aftermath sent shock waves through the city. This historic photo was taken from a balcony of the hotel.

pink-suited Jacqueline ride toward Houston Street in an open car, with Governor John Connally and his wife Nell.

"By the time I returned to the Commerce Street side of the hotel, the TV screen showed a station executive directing questions about where shots had been fired. I sent my food captain, G.T. Montgomery, to see that anyone on the Board with a heart condition had nitroglycerine in hand. Then I announced to the Directors of the Ad League that President Kennedy had been shot.

"There was quite a contrast to the parade scene by 5:00 o'clock," she says "You could have fired a cannon down Main Street and not hit anyone. Downtown Dallas was completely deserted." And in mourning.

After the Kennedy assassination, the Sixties Decade dealt a series of painful blows to almost everyone. The Vietnam War seemed hopeless, and the terms upperclass and establishment were re-defined in the political tensions of the day. The seriousness of the times was reflected in both protest music and entertainment. Black humor became popular. Poetry of the day seemed pointless and alien, except perhaps to the so-called flower children. Long hair, weird clothes, protests, drugs, rock, sit-ins and love-ins became a way of life for many. Place names took on new meaning: Woodstock, San Francisco, Memphis . . . Kent State. Old World grandeur was definitely OUT. The Hotel Adolphus was beginning to look a bit run down at the heels, too, in comparison with several brand new Dallas hotels.

Joe Reichman spotted a new comedienne at Twin Trees, a chic little club out on Lovers Lane. Andy Anderson and Stormy Meadows loved her at first sight. The lady was booked for two weeks in the Century Room. Stormy recalls, "We didn't know anything about her, except that she had a new style and a husband named 'Fang'." It was, of course, that funny lady whose national day, according to Bob Hope, is Halloween: Phyllis Diller. (He can say that; she has been a guest on his specials 23 times, a record.)

Century Room regulars had never seen the likes of Diller's act. Phyllis came springing on stage like a little bird, in a yellow satin suit and gold shoes. Raising her long eyelashes ("They're AWNINGS," she says) to the mirrored ceiling, she looked all around and said, "Wonderful! Even the balcony is full tonight."

* * *

The *creme de la creme* of Century Room stories belongs to the Advertising League of Dallas. Safari '65, the meeting was touted — a big membership drive and luncheon, which brought a record turnout to the meeting. "We had other important business, too," says Joe Crawley, that year's membership chairman. "We were promoting the new downtown bus system, the Dandeliners. To bring the Safari theme and the Dandeliners together, we brought in a live, dandy-lion from Graham, Texas." It was tranquilized, but roared occasionally just to keep everyone happy.

"We had distinguished visitors from the National Advertising Federation," says Crawley, "including our guest speaker, an outstanding woman, who was an ad executive from J. Walter Thompson in Chicago. *Everyone* was there . . . the Mayor, Miss Dallas. KRLD broadcast the whole thing, while Ed Miley captured the meeting on film.

The membership chairman blanches to remember: "Someone motioned that the spotlights were too bright for the speaker to show her slides, so backstage, I found a big button, like a rheostat. I pushed it." The retractable dance floor was set into slow motion. The speaker's table was resting on it.

Horrified, Crawley watched while members, the Mayor, the speakers' table, chairs, the dandy-lion, Miss Dallas, plates of spaghetti, salads, coffee, water and slide show, all went flying.

It was unthinkable, like the San Francisco Earthquake. Fortunately, some brave Ad League member swooped up the speaker, just in time to keep her limbs from being broken, and tossed her up onto the piano. The room looked like a disaster area, but no one was hurt. The lady even made a shaky recovery remark about being bowled over by Texas.

When the ice rink cover rolled back, the sedate luncheon took on a little life.

Now, nearly twenty years later, none of the Ad League members can recall the name of the hero who saved the lady's life. "I thought it was John Rector," says one. But, no, it wasn't, Rector says. "Could it have been Rominger?" asks another. "I'm not sure . . ." No one seems to remember exactly who the hero was; however, they all concur on one point: "It was Joe Crawley who pushed the button!"

Crawley, now an award-winning owner of an agency, laughs to describe the next meeting: "W.W. Aston had fashioned a giant electronic board, flashing with buttons and switches. It was chained on one side to the speaker's stand and to me on the other. I knew then that I'd never live that down."

*   *   *

It was bad news to entertainers when the Century Room was shut down, later in 1965. "I used to daydream about it in Kansas City," says singer Marilyn Maye. "Appearing in the Century Room was wonderful, prestigious, and all I had done up til then was appear in little clubs."

It's too late now, for the Century Room, at least, when

Marilyn comes to Dallas these days. She had to score seven RCA hit albums and seventy-five appearances on the Johnny Carson Show without the Century Room seal of approval. By the time she came back to the Adolphus in 1981 to lend her talents to the New Years Eve revelry, the hotel had been completely renovated. After singing for the second New Year's Eve, by popular demand, Marilyn feels quite at home at the Adolphus . . . so much so that on January 1, 1983, she made chili in the hotel kitchen for the out-of-town troops who followed her for the holiday, "Still," she says with a sigh, "no more Century Room . . ."

* * *

The Aged Lady Begins to Show Her Years

When Hubert Humphrey came to town, he was the first Vice-President to stay overnight since the Kennedy tragedy. With him came the army demolition squad, security guards, and a sharpshooter for every rooftop. The Adolphus staff was startled to find that no one knew how many rooms they needed to check for security, because no one knew how many rooms the hotel had.

"The room number system was unusual from the beginning," says Jo Fischer, "because the first floor started at sub-basement level. Then, the hotel had been through five additions and an undetermined number of alterations. To make matters more complicated, the telephone company put in a new room-dial system, which seemed even more whimsical than the floor numbering system."

Not having any idea how many rooms they had to sell, much less make secure for VIPs, the supervisory staff organized teams to count doors, stairway openings, and the smallest apertures to get an inventory of what the hotel had. They found some unusual features. On the 9th floor, for instance, two 2-room suites seemed to be connected by a door, but the doors on each side opened into a blank wall. A short hallway between the suites had been boarded up and plastered over. The same thing was found on four other floors. "The uncanny part of that," says Jo, "is that each of these boarded-up hallways had been used to store brand-new bedding, mirrors, furniture, etc. The housekeeper, who had been there for thirty years, had never seen it. Hal Fish, the Corrigan purchasing agent, didn't know anything about it." The discovery seemed less strange when they found other surprises, such as stairways leading into blank walls. The Grande Dame seemed to show a sense of humor, but Adolphus Busch would not have been amused.

Stanley Marcus, a man even more renowned for his *Quest for the Best* than Busch, for his uncompromising taste for quality, probably believes that the beer baron would have disapproved all additions to the hotel. Looking back to his boyhood, Marcus is glad he saw the Adolphus in its initial glory. "I remember the hotel from the time I was about twelve years old," he says, "when, frequently, I used to go to the Grill to lunch with my father. The hotel was beautiful then; Adolphus Busch had built it after the fashion of the Blackstone in Chicago. Then, after he died, the family heirs built the additions."

"It was a shame," Marcus continues, "As the years went on, the rooms were divided, changed, and re-divided." At one time, consulting engineers pronounced the hotel impossible to improve with economic feasibility. It would require all new baths and complete renewal on the inside. "It was the worst case of gerrymandering I ever saw," he says, "and the minor changes Corrigan made, long after he bought it, could never correct the problem . . . he simply kept it alive for fifteen more years." But now, with the rooms cut back to 450, the interior completely renewed, and all new plumbing, Marcus says, "They did an extraordinarily fine job."

Managing Director Art Lang came to the hotel in the Seventies when its age weighed heavily upon the hotel. Despite the staff's best efforts, the accommodations had limitations. All baths needed replacement, and Corrigan Properties hesitated to spend millions of dollars to rejuvenate the old downtown hotel building. Dallas was moving in an outward direction, and the Grande Dame was also moving downward and outward.

Tradition and hospitality remained the sole characteristics of the Adolphus which brought people back, over and over, even after the hotels' status had slipped. Some came simply because they had always stayed there; others came because their parents and grandparents had stayed there. It was something personal. One weekend the hotel hosted two couples celebrating their 25th and 35th wedding anniversaries; one couple came all the way from Illinois, the other from El Paso.

The same loyalty prevailed with the staff. A certain laundress had been working there for 47 years. Prosper Ingels had spent 48 in the pastry kitchen. A 30-year old veteran bellman seemed to recognize anyone who had ever been in the hotel before, including a man from Detroit who had been absent for over ten years. The Adolphus was playing the role of the im-

*Manager
Anderson's loyal
staff was a big part
of the hotel's past;
but all wondered
about their future.*

poverished old aristocrat at that point, and her faithful, older
staff helped maintain some degree of dignity.

After Leo Corrigan's death in 1975, the property became an
expensive collector's item, which needed either to have a fortune spent to restore it, or to be sold outright for its scrap
value. No one really wanted the latter. Perhaps the solution
would be to spend *part* of a fortune on the hotel, and *then* sell
it.

When liquor-by-the-drink passed, about forty years after
Frank Harting had prepared the coffee shop for that event, the
time had come to re-open the Century Room. Interior Designer Fred Merrill was contracted to redecorate and refurbish
the lobby areas and other public rooms, the Century Room and
the Handicappers Bar. Under Merrill's direction, the structure
of the original Century Room remained intact, retaining the
mirrored ceiling over the dance floor and a single chandelier
at the entrance. The August 1975 issue of *Texas and Southwest
Hotel-Motel Review* featured a cover story about the new Century Room. It was described as a perfect blend of colors and
fabrics, with walls, columns and bentwood chairs all covered
with layers of suede, and barrel chairs in the adjacent bar
upholstered in a herringbone fabric. The cocoa brown ceiling
and chocolate-colored stage drapery provided a contrast to the
natural finish, basket-weave covering on two side walls.

The Century Room reopened with a bang at the hand of Chris Elson, with an unusual act called "Meteliko." a Hawaiian singer accompanied by five hula girls, a fire/knife drummer named Enoka Fetui, and the Johnny Scat Davis Band.

* * *

When the Andersons came back to the hotel in 1977, Dotty took a hand in redecorating some of the rooms. Just to use some of the old things effectively, she set up a Victorian Room. Andy had the porte cochere's underside stripped of paint down to its solid copper and brass banding and had it polished to a high glow. The Rose Room was beautiful. It set an elegant stage for Ann Anderson's wedding. The hotel's "Eloise" had grown into a lovely young lady by this time.

"Andy Anderson really saw more changes than anyone else over the years," says Dotty Anderson. He had known and met the white glove inspection as a bellhop. He knew how to do hotel routine things like cleaning silver flatware in a machine filled with BBs. He had witnessed a number of the additions and alterations, more rooms, then fewer rooms. Time and the elements had long since changed the copper hue of the Grand Dame's crowning glory to the color of Miss Liberty, right before his eyes.

Things were different now. The slanted marble floor in the lobby had been carpeted. The new microwave oven and the old bottle-crushing machine operated side by side.

However appealing that first redecoration proved to be, it was basically a cosmetic, superficial change. "If they had done it years before,' says Fred Merrill, "they might have stimulated more new interest in the hotel. Without doing other, major changes, however, they still could not compete effectively with the new downtown hotels for convention trade." But at least the redecoration done by Merrill commanded enough attention to the hotel to keep it standing and to attract a buyer.

Each time an old hotel or any colorful old building was razed, Dallas held its breath. The Baker was imploded into a heap of rubble. The green-peaked Medical Arts Building at Pacific and St. Paul was gone, and the nearby Dallas Athletic Club building was marked to disappear. The old Palace Theater on Elm Street had long since been reduced to a parking lot.

The Adolphus could have been lost, surrounded as it was by shiny buildings of metal and multicolored mirrors. The old brick facade, with all its faces and gingerbread, seemed old-fashioned and out of place.

The hotel became the subject of more than one survey as a candidate for preservation as a declared historical landmark. The owners probably had mixed feelings about such a declaration, which would limit their prospective buyers to those interested in it for the building intact. The original tower, plus the series of annexes could become a renewed marvel or, just as easily, a giant millstone around the neck of Dallas. But the Grande Dame triumphed. In 1980, Westgroup, Inc. and the New England Mutual Life Insurance Company bought the Adolphus complex. By that time the hotel was nearly seventy years old and needed *everything*. Their estimated cost for the complete renovation came to $45,000,000, about $42,500,000 more than the price of the original building.

To renew the hotel, the new owners brought together Dallas architects Beran and Shelmire, California interior designer Jill Kurtin Cole of Milton I. Swimmer Planning and Design, Inc., and general contractor Henry C. Beck of Dallas. Together, they created a brand new, grand-old hotel.

The reddish-brown brick and granite were scrubbed and restored to their original appearance. The symbols, faces and figures remained in place. From her antique green head to her red granite toes, the exterior of the hotel was cleaned and freshened, but not changed appreciably. Behind that facade, the interior renovation began, almost from scratch.

Architecture Critic David Dillon wrote in *The Dallas Morning News* on August 23, 1981 that the renovation represented ". . . a bewildering challenge: how to make an elegant new hotel out of an old hodgepodge." Describing the original structure and its semi-related six additions, he said, "Each was drearier than the last and by the time it closed in 1979, the hotel resembled an arrangement of children's blocks."

* * *

Unfortunately, Dillon's words were accurate, but help was on the way. The gap between the garage and the 1918 addition was closed, and the tops knocked off the blocks, in order to create terraces in a stairstep effect. The annex buildings were all plastered a light neutral color to enhance by contrast the old brick. A bright reddish color was used for accent and to link together the alien styles of the buildings.

The old Century Room finally bowed out to a parking garage, with a series of small fountains and garden features in

Renovation Offers New Life and A Dramatic Challenge

the driveway, leading to the registration lobby. Upstairs, the dark-paneled lobby was brightened at the street entrance with an atrium.

Dillon's feature story pointed out that the biggest headache for Beran and Shelmire, the Dallas architects who carried out the renovation, was figuring out how the various parts of the hotel had been assembled. Complete structural drawings existed for only the 1971 West Tower, so the architects constantly found themselves facing beams and columns and other structural surprises. Dillon's description follows:

"Corridors on some of the guest floors are bisected by rows of columns that can't be shifted because they are holding the building up. Other corridors change elevation as they go from one addition to another, or branch off in new and surprising directions, so that guests may be tempted to leave a trail of bread crumbs whenever they leave their rooms."

Still, as Stanley Marcus said, "They did an extraordinarily fine job."

A feature article by Bill Sloan in *Dallas*, the Chamber of Commerce magazine, hailed the Adolphus renaissance as an exception to the trend to eliminate old buildings:

"Two primary factors prevailed in this decision," he wrote. "One of course, is the Adolphus itself. Although 70 years old, it compares to most other old hotels . . . and most new ones, too, for that matter . . . in much the same way as a hand-carved chocolate sculpture compares to a Hershey Bar. From the time it was conceived by Adolphus Busch, the fabulously wealthy beer baron from St. Louis, the Adolphus was pure class." The second factor: ". . . a new company with a revolutionary concept and two of the nation's largest corporate entities, which saw a solid business opportunity in the resurrection of the Adolphus."

Upon completion of the renovation project, a third factor surfaced to assume primary status: "Finally, the involvement of Amfac, Inc., in the management of the 'new' Adolphus provided a framework of expertise and financial strength that would guarantee the rejuvenated hotel's success."

The number of rooms was reduced from 850 to 435. Now the rooms have taken different size and shape, with the smallest having 500 square feet. Terrace suites can connect several bedrooms and baths with a sitting room. The rooms are decorated individually, with luxurious baths befitting the Grande Dame's reputation for hospitality.

The most elaborate arrangement can be found in the penthouse suite with slanted, 10-foot windows, several rooms and a wetbar. Small, round, curtained windows invite a lacy peek at upper Dallas, and the historic bottle-shaped turret hides a closet.

Rare works of art and elegant antiques punctuate the custom-made furnishings to state that this is no ordinary hotel. Two large Flemish tapestries, dated 1661 and signed by G.V.D. Streken, oppose each other across the lobby beneath the new skylight. These are two of an original series of six, dramatizing the life and death of Cleopatra. Several 17th Century Dutch paintings of still life, portraits of majestic types (including Napoleon), and interpretations of mythological figures (Venus and Cupid, and some art nouveau muses) adorn the paneled

Scenic artist and portraitist Alex Rosenfeld paints the French Room murals designed by James L. Frazer of Peter Wolf Concepts.

walls leading into the French Room. The ornately-carved mahogany Victorian grand piano is a pedigreed Steinway. This jewel and other antique pieces defy anyone even to suggest that the Grande Dame's parlor might be a hotel lobby. Enormous arrangements of exotic flowers accent gilt, baroque mirrors and intricately carved, Louis XV wallpieces. Crystals sparkle on *doré* lamps and chandeliers and reflect miscellaneous English pieces intermingled with Oriental tables and decorative pieces.

The project was complete in time for an informal opening in September, 1981, with the formal opening ceremonies scheduled for November. Betty Holloway, Director of Public Relations, had just joined the staff.

"The first hour that the doors were opened," says Betty, "KVIL's Suzie Humphreys drove up in the station's van to cap-

Balloons sailed heavenward, past the unique bottle-shaped tower, on opening day, and the city turned out to honor the Grande Dame's second debut.

ture manager John Kirk. They drove around the Central Business District chatting with air personality Ron Chapman on the radio about the hotel's history." Recalling that Suzie started her career in the Breck Wall production, RAZZ-MA-TAZZ, in 1963, Betty says, "So many media people have sentimental attachments to the old hotel. The series of interviews following Suzie's first interview with Kirk turned out to be very moving."

The November opening was at least four times more grandiose than the hotel's first opening in 1912, and it lasted four times as long. Betty describes it: "We closed the hotel to the public during the exciting four-day celebration. There were already 1,000 people involved. Stephanie May chaired a committee of women active in civic, social and historical organizations to put together a beautiful benefit for KERA (the PBS radio and television stations)."

The champagne started to flow on Friday night, although the spun sugar ribbon wasn't cut by Mayor Jack Evans until the following morning. Dignitaries, the hotel owners, the chefs, hotel department heads, and Amfac representatives gathered beneath a canopy, while a mile-long parade of bands, drill teams, clowns, floats, antique cars, old friends and Santa Claus approached the stand. After a musical ceremony by the Duncanville High School Band, and the ribbon-cutting, a kaleidoscopic array of balloons stormed heaven.

The Saturday gala included afternoon tea in the main lobby and a style show, featuring Carolina Herrera fashions, presented by Lou Lattimore. In the afternoon, guests browsed through Marie Leavell's holiday boutique on the mezzanine and saw a display of Jorge Miguel's fine jewelry. A number of period antique clothes (ca. 1912) were shown by the Dallas Historical Society, including a long, green velvet jacket and skirt, with a gold and green, lace-trimmed chiffon blouse. The garment, with a Neiman-Marcus label, had been worn in 1912 by Mrs. Lawrence Cabell.

The 7:00 P.M. cocktail party preceded a gourmet dinner, followed by dancing to the Peter Duchin orchestra. The rest of the festivities seemed to be one party after another.

During the four-day celebration, special events were arranged for the owners and Amfac managers to become acquainted with the area. Of these, one event took the group to the Bear Creek Resort at Dallas/Ft. Worth Airport; another highlight came with the special fashion show Kim Dawson presented at a luncheon, showing Texas designs.

"When the guests returned to their rooms, they found gifts," says Betty, "Silver perfume bottles (engraved with celebration dates) for the ladies and heavy terry cloth robes (with the hotel logo) for the men. The entire celebration was wonderful!"

*   *   *

Christmas 1981 at the Adolphus saw the beginning of some new traditions. Beneath the skylight, a twenty-five foot white Christmas tree, decorated with strands of silver beads and nosegays in shades of cranberry, stood at the top of the street entrance. The New Year rang into the Grand Ballroom with merriment, just like old times, featuring singer Marilyn Maye, and a menu worthy of St. Sylvestre.

Business-as-usual took a step back to the time when the name Adolphus was synonymous with gracious hospitality. The guest rooms were, once again, large and elegant, with luxurious personal touches. The hotel offered three exceptionally good restaurants in the hotel, and, in addition, afternoon tea and cocktails in the lobby, with music. Concierge Bill Kennedy took his place as one prepared to offer any extra guest services, from chartering a plane to boarding animals. He is one of the few members of *Les Clefs D'Or USA, Ltd.*, a branch of the international concierge organization.

Holiday traditions at the hotel include singer Marilyn Maye, the 25-foot Christmas tree, special pastry creations, and sumptious cuisine from the resident chefs.

General Manager John Kirk, PR Director Betty Holloway, and Chef Consultant Jean Banchet supervise the class, the comfort and the cuisine of the modern Adolphus.

When native New Yorker John Kirk assumed responsibility for re-opening the Adolphus for its second debut in 1981, he was thoroughly acquainted with the delicate balance of old world dignity and modern convenience associated with gracious hotel service. He began his career at the old Waldorf Astoria and the Waldorf Towers in New York, then proceeded to manage newer hotels in Arizona, California and Hawaii.

Mr. Kirk describes the hotel's ideal direction as "Semi-European, combining the old world beauty of the Ritz in London with the warmth of Texas hospitality." In retrospect, he sees the hotel's restoration as a spiritual as well as physical renewal of something that was great in its prime. "The first lustre may be gone," he says, "But a fine, old patina remains in its place."

When Betty Holloway joined the Adolphus staff as Executive Director of Public Relations, shortly before the re-opening in 1981, she brought twenty-five years of experience in public relations. Twelve of those years were spent unrolling the red carpet for VIP guests, celebrities and entertainers, and working with publicity schedules at the Dallas Fairmont Hotel.

In March 1982 *ULTRA* Magazine applauded the Grande Dame's second debut in an article by Derro Evans: "BRAVO, ADOLPHUS! Act IV, Scene I. The beautiful lady with a past has emerged from the wings to once again claim center stage."

General Manager John Kirk accepts the AAA 5-Diamond award honoring the hospitality and cuisine of the new French Room.

Evans traced the dazzling creature's rise as an actress: through the ingenue parts; the ascending star phase; and, the middle age slump.

"But sing no sad songs for the lady in Act IV," wrote Evans. "With fanfare, a ravishing new wardrobe and a legion of new admirers calling at her door, she has emerged as the grande dame, set to charm hearts and conquer horizons in a starring role only age and love could have given her.

"The lady is the Adolphus Hotel back from the depths of a boring, long winter's sleep. The stage is the city of Dallas, in love again . . . as it was in an era beginning 70 years ago . . . with a hotel which learned, with a little help from its friends, how to grow old not merely gracefully, but with grandeur."

The Adolphus and Dallas . . . together again.

The Recipe Collection

Recipes in this collection have been selected from actual restaurant menus found in the French Room, the Grille, the Palm Bar, Afternoon Tea and the pastry kitchen. The dishes are authentic, reduced only in proportion, with their ingredients and quality unchanged.

Some measurements may seem unusual as a result of their presentation here in the American standard cups and spoons, rather than the continental. Nothing has been left out of any recipe in the collection. As one might expect, however, the seasoning measurements are basic suggestions; each chef, and you, must taste for adjustment.

If Adolphus Busch himself could have chosen the Food Services Designer and Consultant Master Chef in the Adolphus, he might have selected Jean Banchet.

Banchet was born in Roanne, France, in 1941. He apprenticed in France in some of the finest restaurants, then moved to London to become chef at the Sporting Club. In the United States, Banchet was encharged with the Playboy Club kitchen, in Geneva, Wisconsin, but left to open his own small, but exclusive restaurant, Le Français , in Wheeling, Illinois. Le Français has been described by the New York Times food critic, Mimi Sheraton, in restaurant superlatives: "This restaurant would have to be exceptional in France," she writes, "and it is among the top half-dozen French restaurants in the United States."

The entire program of menu selection, preparation and presentation of the Adolphus cuisine was outlined and effected by Jean Banchet at the time of the opening in 1981. Banchet continues to come to Dallas each month to maintain uniform quality, train new personnel and oversee the solution of special problems. Essentially, the quality of the highly-rated food services in the hotel is his responsibility.

In the Adolphus kitchen, a combination of French Classical and Country styles has been balanced with the *nouvelle cuisine* to please the most sophisticated palate, for the French Room. In the hotel's Grille Restaurant and Palm Bar, the menu moves toward simplicity, de-escalating in formality, while retaining high standards of excellence.

Banchet's style becomes easily apparent in the French Room, where the menu bears a striking resemblance to the menu of his own restaurant. Attentive waiters, dressed in tuxedo, approach the diners at each table, showing or describing special creations of the evening. Banchet's dramatic presentation of each dish excites the imagination and taste buds before the first bite.

Some of the combinations, such as lobster and mango salad, may appear somewhat unusual to some, but Banchet scorns combinations he considers inappropriate, though they be touted by others as *nouvelle*. The concept of *nouvelle*, to Banchet, embodies clear flavors, lighter sauces, made without flour and little salt.

"Above all," he says, "The most important thing is to use the very best, freshest ingredients. Fish and vegetables, especially, must be cooked only to their peak of perfection."

Banchet's methods and presentation provide the basis of continuity, despite changes of personnel in the hotel. Considering his praiseworthy reputation as an authority on French cuisine, Banchet's enthusiasm is a compliment to the Adolphus kitchen. He says, "This is a first-class operation, and I am proud to continue in the capacity of Chef Consultant." He has predicted that the French Room will take its place among the world's top continental restaurants.

Dishes for the pictures in this book were prepared under the supervision of Michel Cornu and Executive Sous Chef Claude Feracci. Born in Paris, France, Cornu began his apprenticeship in Orleans at 13. His career in hotels and restaurants in France, Switzerland, and the United States has been broken only by service in the French Navy. Cornu came to the Adolphus for its grand re-opening in 1981.

Recipes from the pastry kitchen were prepared by Jean Pierre Piallier for the color photographs in this book. In addition, Piallier has reduced the proportions of all recipes for purposes of home preparation. Each has been tested by him, personally.

In the pastry kitchen, Piallier and his staff of ten cooks begin the day at 3:00 A.M., and work in shifts until the following midnight to supply the hotel restaurants and services with all bread, rolls, croissants, pastry, ice-cream, cakes and other desserts. His decorative pieces are carefully-wrought works of art; some look more like jewelry than pastry.

Piallier began his apprenticeship at 14 at a pastry shop in his native Lyon, France, where he worked twelve-hour shifts, making one thing right after another. "After that, anything I did seemed easy," he says.

In his belief that anything can be done with sugar, Piallier has won gold medals while working in Bermuda and Sri Lanka. He created an incredible, 10-layer wedding cake, with the wedding party descending lacy-bannistered stairs. The bells hung in the cake's steeple, with the bride and groom below, on the first floor layer. The scene was further enhanced in Piallier's style, with cherubs, lights, fountains and flowers.

Recommendations for wine selection by the Adolphus Sommelier have been approved by French Room Manager Michael Hensley. The suggestions accompanying certain recipes in this collection follow the familiar guidelines: white wine to enhance seafood or chicken; red wine for beef or lamb; or, rosé for veal, pork or any of the above. Wine, however, should always be a matter of choice.

A knowledgeable diner may opt for color preference despite menu selection. Wine to accompany light meals, such as soups, salads and sandwiches (as served in the Palm Bar or the Grille Restaurant), should be the kind one enjoys most. Carafe wines do very well for most of these, especially for egg dishes and soups, which tend to neutralize the character of wine.

Many first-course selections on the French Room menu combine seafood or vegetables prepared with white wine. Dishes made with wine should be accompanied by wine of the same color if a special selection is made. No special recommendation is made for a salad course. The wine chosen to accompany the entrée should be on the table by that time. However, if a separate wine *is* taken, wine color-matched to the dressing vinegar will lend itself to the flavor.

For the true sophisticate who enjoys Port and other dessert wines, a few recommendations are included. Remember, that when in doubt, good champagne and expensive chocolates seal your reputation as a thoughtful host.

The French Room

The French Room

For the second time, the French Room's beauty has become the talk of the town and beyond. In Adolphus Busch's day, its elegance was legendary, with a mirrored fountain, wrought bronze balustrade and walls of Breccia Violette marble. The French Room provided strong contrast to other restaurants in Dallas. Nothing in the neighboring Oriental Hotel was any match for it, and, certainly, the pale, rustic block of storefronts around the two hotels offered no other basis for comparison.

The French Room's original beauty and its current decor seem even more fascinating now, in an era which has by-passed gilt and rococo for functional metal and glass. Soft colors on the French Room floor have been woven to match the muraled walls. The same pastel colors accent two enormous Venetian glass chandeliers, offsetting golden swirls and hops on arches and a vaulted ceiling. Windows have been draped in rose to complement upholstery on Louis XVI armchairs.

Some romantic figures, cherubim, flower garlands, and clouds were painted directly on the walls and high ceiling from scaffolding, in the manner of Michelangelo, while others were painted on canvas and attached. The design came from the creative hand of James L. Frazer and Peter Wolf Concepts.

To underscore the quality of a menu which is, perhaps, the room's most striking feature, dining tables are covered with beige moire taffeta and set with fine crystal and china. The French Room rates the full five stars from restaurant critics. Its cuisine, established by food artist Jean Banchet, is carried forward by two chefs: Pascal Gode and Pascal Vignau, who have become known affectionately as "The Two Pascals."

Perfection in dining demands more than beautifully prepared dishes in the French Room. The menu embodies a balance of strong and light flavors, colors and textures. Take Jean Banchet's advice about using the best quality ingredients you can afford and the freshest . . . and then cook them just to the peak of their perfection.

The subtle flavors combined in this cold soup make it a favorite of Pascal Vignau.

ARTICHOKE AVOCADO SOUP   *Serves 4*

2 tablespoons butter
4 large artichokes
1 leek
1 onion
1 medium potato, peeled and cubed
1½ quarts chicken stock
1 pint cream, reduced to half its volume
2 avocados (1 for soup, 1 for garnish)

Clean and trim artichokes. Remove 10 big leaves, blanch them in salted water and save for decoration. Cut artichokes into 4-6 segments. Clean and slice leek and onion. Cook them with artichokes in butter over low heat, just until soft and yellow. Add the potato and cook five minutes. Add chicken stock. Cook 20 minutes and puree the mixture in a blender. Reduce cream to half volume by cooking directly over low heat eight minutes. Add the puree to the cream. Add the avocado and press all through a strainer. Chill before serving. Place a slice of avocado and the artichoke leaves on the side of soup plates.

In the French Room, beauty and color rank in importance with flavor as appetite stimulants. This colorful vegetable terrine, cooked and chilled a day ahead, is appealing, but difficult, and requires a food processor and electric knife.

Vegetable Terrine

Seafood Ballottine

VEGETABLE TERRINE

Serves 4

1 carrot
1 zucchini squash
1 yellow squash
10 mushrooms
6 artichoke hearts
1 large flowerhead of broccoli
1 pound fresh asparagus, tips only

1 pint cold, heavy cream
1 whole egg
1 pound raw chicken or veal (or ½ pound each), very cold
Salt and pepper

Serve with a dry white wine, such as a Chablis, a Mâcon, or a Pouilly-Fuissé.

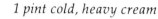

Slice mushrooms and artichoke hearts vertically. Cut vegetables into sticks and slivers and blanch in boiling, salted water. Drain, cool in ice water and drain on paper towel. Layer vegetables in a terrine or loaf pan to contrast colors. Grind chicken to small pieces and blend to a paste in the processor with the egg, salt and pepper. Add cream slowly and mix thoroughly to heavy cream consistency. Pour over the vegetables and bake in a Bain Marie at 225° for 1½ hours, or until firm. Cool and refrigerate overnight. Remove from terrine and slice with electic knife.

ASPARAGUS WITH MUSTARD SAUCE

Serves 4

36 large spears of fresh asparagus
1 teaspoon fresh basil, chopped
Salt and pepper

Mustard Sauce:

2 shallots
1 teaspoon butter
1 cup white wine
1 tablespoon sherry vinegar
1 pint cream
2 tablespoons Dijon mustard
Blanched red pepper strips for garnish

Peel the asparagus. Cut away the stems and save. Cook the tips in a steamer and set aside. Boil the stems, drain and purée. Blend with basil, salt and pepper. To make the sauce, chop shallots and sauté them in a saucepan with melted butter. Cook slowly over low heat. Do not brown. When tender, add white wine and vinegar and reduce to ½ volume. Add cream and reduce again to ½ volume. Strain and add mustard. (Mustard Seed Sauce may be used. See recipe in Sauce Section.) To serve, allow 9 tips to each small plate and a mound of puree. Pour sauce around the plate and over the tips. Garnish with strips of red bell pepper.

Serve with a flavorful wine, such as an Alsatian Gewürztraminer, or even a Cru Beaujolais from Fleurie or Brouilly.

Seafood Ballottine, with its exotic ingredients, typifies the elegance of the French Room.

SEAFOOD BALLOTTINE   *Serves 10-12*

1 3-pound side of salmon, pounded flat
⅔ cup scallops with roe
⅔ cup lobster meat
2 ounces sea urchins
1 small eel, smoked
3 leaves dry seaweed
1 ounce cognac

1 recipe lobster mousse
1 recipe scallop mousse

Lobster Mousse:

1 pound lobster
1 egg
1 quart cream
¼ cup reduced fish stock
Salt, pepper

Scallop Mousse:

½ pound scallops
1 egg
1 pint cream
¼ cup reduced fish stock
Salt, pepper

Decorated Tray with Vegetable Terrine and Seafood Ballottin

Prepare lobster and scallop mousses separately for rolled ballottine. Grind the lobster and scallops for the mousses the day before and keep refrigerated; meat must be very cold before blending in the food processor. To each, add eggs, salt and pepper and blend to a paste. Add cream slowly and mix to the thickness of heavy cream. Correct seasonings and set each mousse aside.

Serve with a medium-bodied white Graves, a California Chardonnay, or, possibly, a Meursault.

Mix the lobster mousse with scallops, lobster meat, sea urchins, chives and cognac. Flatten salmon slice and spread with ¼″ thickness of scallop mousse, then a layer of seaweed leaves. Cover the leaves with lobster mousse and stretch the eel across the center. Roll up carefully. Wrap tightly in buttered aluminum foil. Bake in *bain marie* at 275° for 45 minutes. Remove from foil. Cool and slice for serving.

Ballottine of Salmon is really an adaptation of the Seafood Ballottine served in the French Room. Pascal Vignau recommends it for home preparation for those who don't have sea urchins, smoked eel and seaweed on hand. A salmon mousse is substituted for the lobster mousse for practicality.

BALLOTTINE OF SALMON   *Serves 10-12*

1 side of salmon, skinned and boned
1½ pounds mussels
½ pound scallops with roe
½ pound lobster meat
2 bunches chopped chives (3 tsp. dried)
1 bunch chopped tarragon (1 tsp. dried)
2 sheets dry seaweed or 10-15 large spinach leaves

1 recipe salmon mousse
1 recipe scallop mousse

Salmon Mousse:

1 pound salmon
1 egg
1 quart cream
Salt and pepper

Scallop Mousse:

½ pound scallops
1 egg
1 pint cream
Salt and pepper

To make a good mousse, begin with very cold ingredients. Do not mix more than 5 minutes. Follow the same procedure for each mousse. Put diced salmon (or scallops) into the food processor with egg. Mix to an elastic paste, then add cream slowly.

To assemble Ballottine, split the side of salmon, butterfly style, into a big sheet ¼″ thick. Spread upside down on plastic wrap. Cover the salmon with scallop mousse. Spread with seaweed or spinach leaves.

Mix the mussels, scallops, lobster, chives and tarragon with the salmon mousse, adding salt and pepper to taste. Spread the mixture over the seaweed and roll salmon like a jelly roll. Wrap in plastic, then in foil twisting ends tightly. Cook in simmering water for 45 minutes. If you have a thermometer, the inside temperature should reach 125°. A small skewer should insert easily. Remove the Ballottine from foil. Cool and slice for serving.

Serve with a light, delicate wine, such as a Muscadet, Pouilly Fumé, white Bordeaux, or an Italian Soave.

A colorful accompaniment to the French Room dining experience is the three vegetable mousse made in muffin tin molds. The recipe could become your favorite do-ahead vegetable for buffets.

THREE VEGETABLE MOUSSE

Serves 15-20

Spinach Layer:

1½ pounds spinach
3 tablespoons butter
3 eggs
Salt and pepper

Clean and sauté the spinach with 2 tablespoons of the butter, the salt and pepper. Squeeze out cooking juices and put the spinach in a food processor or blender with remaining table-spoon of butter and the eggs. Blend until it has a thick paste consistency. Set aside.

Carrot Layer:

   1 pound carrots
   2 tablespoons butter
   1 cup cream
   2 eggs

Cut carrots into small pieces and cook in salted water until tender. Drain water and dry out the carrots by placing the pan in a 150° oven for 15 minutes. Blend carrots with butter, cream and eggs to a paste consistency. Set aside.

Turnip Layer:

   1 pound turnips
   2 tablespoons butter
   1 cup cream
   2 eggs

Follow the method for preparing carrot layer to prepare the turnips. To assemble the mousse, spoon a layer of each vegetable into buttered muffin tins or similar molds measuring 2½" across. Bake very slowly at 250° in a *bain marie* for 1½ hours. Unmold on a tray or baking sheet and reheat just before serving.

Fresh herbs in a special marinade add flavor to this favorite of Pascal Gode.

SALMON SALAD   *Serves 4-6*

   1 side of fresh small salmon, boned
   1 head limestone lettuce
   1 head endive with red leaves
   2 hardcooked eggs
   Cherry tomato halves for garnish

Marinade:

3 cups olive oil
Juice of 10 limes
Juice of 4 lemons
7 teaspoons salt
2 teaspoons pepper
Tarragon to taste, reserve a few leaves for garnish
1 bunch thyme
1 bunch dill
1 bunch chervil

Dressing:

1 cup olive oil
Juice of 2 limes
Juice of 2 lemons
Salt and pepper to taste

Combine marinade ingredients in bowl large enough to hold salmon. Add salmon to marinade and let stand for six hours, turning every 45 minutes. To make dressing, combine olive oil, lime and lemon juice, salt and pepper. Mix well and set aside. When ready to serve, line salad plates with the lettuce. Toss the endive with the dressing and divide it among the plates. Remove salmon from marinade, draining well. Slice salmon into very thin scallops and arrange them on top of the endive. Garnish with a few cherry tomatoes and chopped hardcooked egg. Add a few fresh tarragon leaves and serve.

FRENCH ROOM SALAD

Make your own salad of favorite lettuce greens and other leafy or crisp vegetable combinations, adding anything you wish which goes with a vinaigrette dressing. Base your decision on freshness and availability of attractive vegetables. Toss with a dressing of ½ cup olive oil and ¼ cup fresh lemon juice, seasoned with salt and pepper. Or you may use the *Vinaigrette Dressing* in the Sauce and Dressing section. To each serving, add one hot, 2 ounce portion of *crottin de chavignol*, heated briefly under a 450° broiler. This goat milk cheese always accompanies the French Room Salad, along with four plain, toasted croutons.

PEA SOUP

Serves 6

1 leek
½ cup onions
3 ounces prosciutto
14 ounces frozen peas
2 quarts chicken stock
2 langostino tails, broiled, or
1 pound Littleneck clams, steamed

Chop leek and onions and dice prosciutto. Sauté together in 1½ tablespoons butter. Add peas and sauté two minutes. Add chicken stock and cook until peas are soft, about 10 minutes. Blend in processor. Serve garnished with broiled langostinos or Littleneck clams.

CUISSES de GRENOUILLES au PARFUM de PROVENCE

Serves 4 (appetizer)
Serves 2 (main course)

2 dozen frog legs, soaked and blotted dry
4 cups chopped fresh tomatoes, cooked
¾ cup prepared snail butter
Chopped fresh parsley
Lemon stars for garnish

Serve with a Pouilly Fumé from the Loire Valley, an Italian Verdicchio, or a California Sauvignon Blanc.

Frog legs aren't spur of the moment fare. People who enjoy eating them expect to spend some time in their preparation. The legs are the only edible part of a frog, and are purchased already dressed. Skewer the legs and soak them in cold water for several hours, changing water every two hours. Prepare Butter for *Snails à la Bourguignonne*. Cook fresh, chopped tomatoes.

Sauté frog legs a few at a time in ½ cup snail butter. Put six on each plate and baste with remaining butter. Top with chopped, cooked tomatoes. Sprinkle with chopped parsley and decorate with lemon.

Each serving allows three pairs per appetizer, or six pairs per main course.

Butter for Snails à la Bourguignonne   *Makes 1 Cup*

  ¾ cup unsalted butter
  ¼ cup finely chopped shallots
  ½ clove garlic, pounded to paste
  1 teaspoon salt
  ⅛ teaspoon pepper

Mix ingredients together by hand.

GRATIN LANGOSTINOS   *Serves 1*

Serve with a white Burgundy or a California Chardonnay.

  1 whole langostino
  6 medium langostino tails
  1 handful of fresh spinach
  2 ounces of Nantua sauce (see Sauce section)
  1 ounce Hollandaise sauce (see Sauce section)
  1 ounce whipped cream
  2 tablespoons butter

Sauté langostinos very lightly in butter, then sauté the spinach leaves using the same pan. In a cassolette, arrange the spinach leaves on the bottom and cover with the langostino tails. Mix the Nantua, whipped cream and Hollandaise together and pour over all. Glaze under the broiler till slightly brown and bubbly. Decorate with the whole langostino and serve.

LOBSTER WITH MANGO SALAD   *Serves 1*

Serve with an Alsace Riesling, a white Bordeaux, or a Chablis.

  1 lobster tail, poached in water, salt and pepper
  1 mango
  1 handful mixed green salad
  1 slice of truffle
  Several leaves of fresh basil
  Truffle Vinaigrette

Slice the lobster and the mango in lengthwise strips of matchstick thickness. Season the salad and arrange on a plate.

Pea Soup with Langostinos, and Assorted Soups

Lobster with Mango Salad

Over the salad, place alternating layers of lobster and mango. Garnish with basil leaves and julienne strips of lemon zest. Make Truffle Vinaigrette by combining 1 tablespoon walnut oil, 1 teaspoon truffle juice and 1 teaspoon Xeres vinegar. Encircle salad and a ring of Vinaigrette and garnish the lobster with a truffle slice on top.

SQUAB WITH PÉRIGOURDINE

Serves 4

4 squab, 12 ounces each, boned
8 baby carrots with tops
2 zucchini, cut in thin strips with skin
1 cup Périgourdine sauce (see Sauce section)

Serve the squab and quail dishes with a red Burgundy, a Napa Cabernet, or a St. Emilion Bordeaux.

Sauté the squab in 1 tablespoon browned butter. Add 1 tablespoon clarified butter. Bake for 12 minutes in a 450° oven until medium rare. Slice each squab into five pieces. Arrange the slices in stairstep fashion. Pour Périgourdine sauce over all and garnish with raw vegetables.

QUAIL WITH HONEY VINEGAR

Serves 1

3 boneless quail
2 ounces duck mousse
1 ounce canned duck liver
2 ounces butter
2 ounces quail juices
1 ounce honey vinegar
2 ounces Demi-glaze (see Sauce section)
1 quail egg
1 timbale of Vegetable Mousse

To make duck mousse, begin with 1 pound of cold duck, blended to a paste in the processor with 1 egg, salt and pepper. Add 1 pint cream slowly and mix to a thick consistency. Dice the duck liver and mix with 2 ounces of the mousse. Stuff quail with the mousse, holding them together with toothpicks in each end. Sauté the quail in 1 ounce butter for 10 minutes. Place on a plate with the vegetable timbale in the center. Sauté the quail egg until firm. Place on top of the vegetable timbale. Add honey vinegar to the pan juices to deglaze. Add the Demi-glaze and 1 ounce of butter. Pour sauce over quail and serve.

Here's one for the hunter. The duck mousse stuffing used for the quail is the same recipe found in the Quail with Honey Vinegar. If you need only a few ounces, make half the mousse recipe for stuffing quail for either dish.

ASSIETTE de la FERME   Serves 4

2 ounces duck mousse (See Quail with Honey Vinegar)
2 tablespoons clarified butter
4 breasts of duck
2 squab, 14 ounces each
2 quail, boned
3 ounces canned goose liver pâté
1 ounce spinach, either sautéed or cooked with water
1 cup white wine
1 small carrot, chopped
½ medium onion, chopped
2 shallots, chopped
1 sprig of thyme
2 tablespoons unsalted butter, cold
2 cups Demi-glaze
Salt and pepper to taste

Serve with a light red Burgundy, such as a Beaujolais-Villages.

Begin by making the duck mousse. If possible, grind the meat for it the day before and keep it very cold in the refrigerator. To clarify the 2 tablespoons butter, melt it very slowly and strain off white residue. Sauté squab and breasts of duck to golden brown in a heavy skillet. Mix the pâté, diced, the chopped spinach, and the duck mousse and stuff the quails, closing each end with a toothpick, then sauté quails in the skillet with the squab and duck.
Place all in a pre-heated 375° oven, removing each after its

Squab with Perigourdine

Quail with Honey Vinegar

cooking time: the quails, after 7 minutes; the duck and squab after 10 minutes.

Remove birds to serving plate and keep them warm. Transfer cooking fat to a saucepan, add 1 tablespoon butter, carrot, shallots, onions and thyme. Take the squab off the bones, leaving the meat on the serving plate. Chop the bones with a heavy knife and add them to the saucepan. Cook over low heat for 10 minutes. Deglaze pan with white wine, reducing ⅔, then add the Demi-glaze. Strain the sauce, then stir in remaining tablespoon butter, and salt and pepper to taste. Cut the duck and squab in very thin slices and arrange in a fan on each plate. Cut the quails in half and place one half in the center of each plate. Pour the sauce around the plate, rather than over the birds. Garnish the plate with any vegetables for color and serve.

This must be the zenith of all filet mignon preparations:

TOURNEDOS SAUTÉ aux TRUFFES   *Serves 4*

A Cabernet Sauvignon is very suitable, and will not overshadow the flavors of the sauce.

4 8-ounce filets
1 tablespoon truffle juice
1 ounce truffles
1 cup Madeira
1 cup Port
3 tablespoons butter
2 cups Demi-glaze (see Sauces)
3 shallots, chopped
1 sprig thyme

Sauté the filets to desired doneness in a skillet in 2 tablespoons of the butter. Remove the filets and add chopped shallots. Deglaze the skillet with the Port. Add thyme and reduce by half. Add the Demi-glaze and cook for 5 minutes. Pour in the Madeira and continue to cook until the sauce is slightly thick. Add the truffle juice for flavor and strain. Add the remaining tablespoon of butter. Pour the sauce over the filets and garnish with truffle slices.

SALMON TOURNEDOS

Serves 4

8 4-ounce slices salmon
25 green peppercorns
25 pink peppercorns
1 cup white wine
1 quart cream
1 shallot, chopped
Salt and pepper

Steam salmon, either in a steamer or on a stainless rack in a large pot using the wine for liquid. Add a few peppercorns of each color. After 8 or 10 minutes, remove the salmon. Reduce the liquid to a syrup. Add remaining peppercorns, shallot and cream. Reduce to the consistency of a sauce. Cover the serving plate with the sauce and arrange salmon slices in a flower shape.

GRENADIN de VEAU aux CHANTERELLES

Serves 4

8 3-ounce medallions of veal
2 tablespoons butter
1½ cup white wine
1 quart cream
8 oz. chanterelles
2 tablespoons clarified butter
2 bunches of chives, chopped
Salt and pepper to taste

Serve with a light red Burgundy from the Côte de Beaune region, or a full-bodied white Burgundy from Meursault or Montrachet.

Sauté medallions in 2 tablespoons butter in a skillet to desired doneness. Remove veal from pan and deglaze the skillet with white wine. Reduce ⅔, add the cream and continue to reduce sauce to a slightly thickened consistency. Clarify remaining 2 tablespoons butter by melting slowly and straining off white deposit. Sauté the washed and cut chanterelles until golden brown, but still firm. Add the chanterelles to the cream sauce. Cook for three minutes, then add chives, salt and pepper. Pour sauce over the medallions and serve.

ZEPHIR GRENOUILLES

Serves 4

2 dozen frog legs
½ pound scallops, cold
1 egg
2 shallots
¼ cup white wine
1 ounce butter
3 ounces chopped sorrel
1 quart cream
Salt and pepper

Make a mousse with scallops, egg and half the cream. Place scallops and egg in the processor to make a paste. Add cream slowly. Sauté frog legs and remove the bones. Set bones aside. Mix the frogleg meat into the mousse by hand. Spoon mixture into eight medium size buttered muffin cups or molds. Bake in *bain marie* at 250° for 15 or 20 minutes. Serve two on each plate. To make sorrel sauce, chop the shallots and sauté in butter with the frog leg bones. Add white wine to deglaze. Remove bones. Reduce volume by ⅔. Add the cream and reduce again by ⅓ or until creamy. Blend with chopped sorrel in a mixer, then strain and serve over the baked Zephir Mousse.

HARICOTS VERTS DUCK LIVER

Serves 4

A dry Riesling, or possibly a Sauvignon Blanc or a Chardonnay, goes well with this.

1 canned duck liver
1 shallot
1 tablespoon Xeres vinegar
1 tablespoon walnut oil
1 ounce truffle peeling
1 pinch chervil
9 ounces French string beans
Salt and pepper
Vinaigrette dressing

Blanch the string beans until *al denté*. Set aside. Cut the duck liver into ¼" slices. Chop the shallots. In a skillet without fat, brown the duck liver until golden brown on each side. Remove from the fire. Cook shallot in the same skillet, add vinegar and cook for one minute. Add salt, pepper, chervil and truffle peeling. Remove from heat. Add the walnut oil and remove the sauce to a bowl, but keep it warm. Sauté the string beans for one minute in one ounce of butter just to warm them. Serve on a warmed plate with the duck liver over the string beans. Pour vinaigrette around the string beans.

FEUILLANTINE de RIS de VEAU

Serves 4

2 pairs sweetbreads
1 ounce white vinegar
Few sprigs of parsley
1 stalk celery
2 tablespoons butter
5 shallots, chopped
1½ cup dry Vermouth
1 quart cream
5 basil leaves
Salt and pepper to taste

8 ounces puff paste (See Pastry section)

Serve a Meursault or a Puligny-Montrachet.

Soak sweetbreads in cold water for 1 hour. Drain, add vinegar, celery, parsley, and enough water to cover. Cook to the boiling point, then simmer for 10 minutes. Drain and plunge immediately into ice water. When cold, trim off any tube, cartilage and fat.

Place sweetbreads in a heavy skillet with the butter and cook over low heat until golden brown on both sides. Add shallots and cook for 5 minutes. Add the vermouth and reduce to half. Stir in cream and seasoning, cover, and allow to cook for 15 minutes. Remove the sweetbreads and reduce the sauce until slightly thick. Mix the sauce, chopped basil, salt and pepper in a blender.

Roll out puff pastry to ¼-inch thickness and bake on a baking sheet in a 400° oven, turning once to make each side golden brown. Then cut the pastry in 3-inch squares, slicing each square into two layers. Place sweetbreads (cut to fit) on bottom layers, pour sauce over, and cover each with the top layer of the pastry square. Place the remaining pieces of sweetbreads around the plate in the sauce.

RACK OF LAMB PERSILLADE

Rack of Four Chops

1 small rack of lamb
2 teaspoons Dijon mustard
1 cup bread crumbs
½ teaspoon salt
½ teaspoon pepper
3 garlic cloves, crushed
1 twig fresh thyme
1 tablespoon olive oil
1 cup chopped parsley

Any of the flavorful Bordeaux wines will be good with the Lamb.

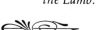

To make persillade, combine all ingredients except lamb and mustard in a processor. Process, allowing mixture to stay very green. Do not over process. Roast the rack of lamb at 450° for 20 minutes (medium rare). Five minutes before removing from oven, brush with Dijon mustard and persillade. Serve the rack with natural lamb juices.

The Grille

The Grille is the hotel's all-encompassing restaurant, serving morning, noon and night. Neither as formal as the evening French Room nor as informal as the daytime Palm Bar, the Grille offers a complete menu including the best of both worlds.

The salads are spectacular and the desserts are works of art. The soup changes daily, but the famous onion soup is always available. In addition to the written menu, there is a spoken menu describing dishes created especially for the day. One of the most popular items on the menu is an appetizer, which can also be ordered as an entrée.

PETITE FRICASSÉE PROVENÇALE   *Serves 4*

    4 squares puff pastry (see Pastry section)
    8 ounces Demi-glaze (see Sauces section)

    8 ounces butter
    1 pound raw spinach, chopped
    6 ounces mushrooms, sliced
    8 artichoke hearts, halved
    ½ teaspoon chopped garlic
    1 teaspoon chopped, fresh parsley
    Salt and pepper to taste

This dish goes well with a dry Rosé, a light-bodied Italian white wine, or a white Bordeaux.

Sauté spinach in 1 ounce of butter. Split pastry, laying tops aside, and place spinach in the center of each. Sauté mushrooms and artichoke hearts in 3 ounces of butter, then remove from the pan. Add garlic, parsley, salt and pepper to the pan with the Demi-glaze. Cook to reduce to ½ its volume. Stir in remaining 4 ounces butter. Place the mushrooms over the spinach and replace pastry tops. Arrange four artichoke halves on each dish beside the pastry. Pour sauce around the puff pastry and serve at once.

Rack of Lamb Persillade
(inset) Haricots Vert Duck Liver

Here are two soup favorites from Ed Hubbard, who makes all soups for the Adolphus.

GAZPACHO   *Serves 6*

1 green pepper
1 red pepper
3 fresh tomatoes, peeled and seeded
4 cucumbers, peeled and seeded
1 finely chopped onion
1 clove garlic
1 cup tomato juice
3 tablespoons lemon juice
1 ounce olive oil
1 teaspoon sweet basil
1 teaspoon tabasco
3 teaspoons oregano
Salt and white pepper to taste

Chop tomatoes, cucumbers, peppers, onion and garlic, almost to a puree. Add tomato and lemon juice, then spices. Finish by stirring in olive oil and seasoning to taste with salt and pepper. Chill before serving.

LOBSTER BISQUE   *Serves 10*

½ cup diced carrots
½ cup chopped celery
½ cup onion
½ cup chopped shallots
¼ cup brandy
2 cups white wine
3 pounds lobster heads
3 quarts fish stock
1 cup tomato paste
1 quart heavy cream
4 ounces butter
Thyme, bay leaves, parsley, salt and pepper to taste

Sauté the carrots, celery and onion with the lobsters in two ounces of butter. Add tomato paste and let it cook for 1 minute with lobster to allow the acidity of the tomato to evaporate.

Then add brandy and flambé. Add white wine and boil down to about half the volume. Add spices, herbs and the fish stock. Reduce all to ⅓ of its volume. Add cream and cook ten more minutes. Strain through a sieve, pressing the vegetables through the mesh. Break and mash the shells in the strainer to extract their juice, then discard the shells. Blend in remaining butter.

Tim Paige, Sous Chef in charge of the Grille cuisine, offers his own favorite recipe.

BALLOTTINE OF CAPON WITH VEAL MOUSSE *7 Slices*

4 double breasts of capon
16 large leaves of spinach
1 pound veal tenderloin
2 eggs
8 ounces heavy whipping cream
½ ounce truffle peelings
1 large shallot, chopped
½ bunch fresh chives
Salt and white pepper to taste

¾ cup Mustard Seed sauce
⅓ cup Hollandaise
⅓ cup whipped cream

A California Chardonnay or French white Burgundy will add to the enjoyment of this Capon.

Place each double breast of capon between 2 sheets of plastic wrap and pound flat, about ⅛" thick. Remove wrap. Wilt spinach leaves with ¼ cup butter and place one layer of leaves over the surface of the capon breasts. Prepare and spread Veal Mousse, about ¼" thick. To make mousse, puree the veal in a food processer. Add 2 eggs and spin for a few seconds till the eggs are mixed. Slowly add the heavy cream. When half the cream has been added, mix in the chives, shallots, truffle peelings and salt and pepper. Continue pouring the cream till a smooth consistency is achieved. Adjust seasonings. After spreading the mousse over the capon, roll lengthwise into an elongated, loaf shape. Wrap with plastic and poach in simmering salted water about 11 to 14 minutes. Remove from water, take off plastic wrap, and slice into seven medallions. Arrange

The Grille

on a dinner plate, with six around one center medallion. Combine Mustard Seed sauce, Hollandaise and whipped cream. Top with sauce and place under the broiler to brown lightly. Garnish with parsley sprigs.

From the brunch menu in the Grille, this dish has a Spanish accent. It combines eggs with eggplant and delicious seasonings.

HUEVOS BERENJENA   *Serves 4*

1 medium eggplant, cut in 8 slices
8 poached eggs
¼ cup butter
1 onion, plus 2 shallots, chopped
1 cup white wine
1 pint cream
2 chopped, fresh tomatoes
2 ounces tomato puree
¼ teaspoon cilantro
¼ teaspoon minced garlic
¼ teaspoon oregano
1 jalapeno pepper, chopped
Salt and pepper to taste
⅛ teaspoon cayenne

To Prepare Eggplant, dip slices in flour, then into a mixture of two egg yolks and two tablespoons of milk, then dip in dry bread crumbs. Fry quickly in 1 cup salad oil, turning once. Drain on a paper towel and keep warm.

Sauce: Sauté onions and shallots in butter, add white wine and cook, reducing to the consistency of syrup. Add fresh tomatoes, cream, cilantro, garlic, oregano, and cook to reduce liquid to ⅓ of the volume. Remove from heat, add tomato puree, jalapeno pepper, cayenne, salt and pepper. Mix all in a blender and strain.

To Assemble: Poach eggs. Place two slices of the fried eggplant on each plate with a poached egg on each slice. Top with the sauce and serve at once.

COLD CUCUMBER SOUP

Serves 10

4 cucumbers
2 potatoes
½ gallon chicken stock
1 pint whipping cream
2 teaspoons dill
Salt, pepper
2 ounces butter

Peel and seed cucumbers; peel potatoes. Cut cucumbers and potatoes into several pieces and heat together in a pan with the butter. Do not let them brown. Add chicken stock, salt, pepper and dill. Cook for twenty minutes. Blend all together with a mixer or blender and allow the mixture to cool. Add the cream and adjust the seasoning. Chill before serving.

EGGS SARDOU

Serves 1

Prepare Spinach

1 pound clean, chopped spinach
½ cup heavy cream
½ cup Béchamel sauce
2 tablespoons butter
Nutmeg, salt and pepper

Sauté spinach in butter. In a separate pan, reduce the cream to half its volume by cooking slowly over low heat, stirring constantly for about 5 minutes. Add Béchamel sauce and spices. Add spinach to the sauce.

To Assemble Eggs Sardou

2 artichoke bottoms
2 poached eggs
2 ounces Hollandaise sauce
2 slices of truffle
Baked pie crust the size of serving dish

Spread the spinach over the crust. Place the artichoke bottoms in the center and set the poached eggs on top. Pour Hollandaise over the eggs and place a slice of truffle on top of each.

Petite Fricassee Provençale

Eggs Sardou

CREAM OF WATERCRESS SOUP   *Serves 6 small portions*

4 tablespoons butter
12 ounces, or 2 bunches watercress
½ medium onion, diced
1 medium potato, peeled and sliced
1 branch of celery, sliced
1 leek, white section only, sliced
4 cups chicken stock
4 ounces heavy cream
Bouquet Garni: *Wrap and tie in a small square of cheesecloth*
    ⅛ teaspoon each of thyme and rosemary and ½ bay leaf
Salt and pepper to taste

Melt 2 tablespoons butter and sauté watercress stems, onion, celery and leek in a large saucepan. Add stock, potato and *bouquet garni* and cook until potato is tender. In a separate pan, sauté watercress leaves in remaining butter, just until wilted, but retaining color. Remove the cloth from the stock and add watercress to stock mixture. Puree in blender and strain. Allow to chill in refrigerator. When cold, stir in heavy cream and add salt and pepper to taste. Serve cold.

AVOCADO SEAFOOD SALAD   *Serves 1*

½ avocado
¼ head limestone lettuce, leaves separated
⅓ tomato
4 medium size shrimp
2 ounces sliced mushrooms
1 ounce mayonnaise mixed with ½ ounce sour cream
2 crab claws
4 ounces crabmeat
1 ounce Bay scallops
1 ounce Louis Dressing (see Dressing section)
¼ lemon
1 split black olive

Mix crabmeat and scallops with Louis Dressing. Mix slices of mushroom with sour cream and mayonnaise. Arrange on plate as shown in picture.

SALADE NIÇOISE

Serves 1

3 ounces boiled potato, diced
3 ounces white tuna
3 ounces French string beans, cooked
4 slices tomato
2 slices of hard-cooked egg
2 black olives
2 fillets of anchovies
2 ounces shredded lettuce
¼ head Boston lettuce

Chill all ingredients before assembling. Arrange as shown in picture. Dress with vinaigrette.

GRILLE CHEF SALAD

Serves 1

1½ ounces turkey in julienne strips
1½ ounces ham, julienned
1½ roast beef strips
1½ ounces Gruyère cheese in strips
2 scallions, strips
2 black olives
1 ounce shredded red cabbage
½ head limestone lettuce
A few spinach leaves

Start with the limestone lettuce laid flat and spread like a fan. Add the shredded cabbage and spinach leaves. Arrange julienne strips in a starburst to match the picture. Serve with your choice of salad dressing.

VEAL SALTIMBOCCA

Serves 1

2 3-ounce scallops of veal
2 slices prosciutto
4 dry sage leaves
¼ cup lemon juice
¼ cup butter
1 ounce Demi-glaze (see Sauces section)

Chef Salad and Salad Nicoise

Prepare veal by rubbing with sage leaves. Place a slice of prosciutto on each. Dust veal side with flour. Sauté in butter, ham side first. Remove from pan. Deglaze the pan with lemon juice and Demi-glaze. Pour over veal.

RAINBOW TROUT   *Serves 4*

4 10-ounce trout
1½ teaspoons chopped shallots
1½ teaspoons chopped parsley
3 ounces diced, cooked ham
1 cup white wine
1 cup cream
1 teaspoon mixed herbs (bay leaf, thyme, oregano)
Salt and pepper to taste
3 tablespoons melted butter

Try a Mosel wine, or an Alsace Riesling, with this one.

Place trout in generously buttered baking dish and brush with melted butter. Sprinkle with salt, pepper, diced ham, shallots, parsley and herbs. Add white wine and bake for 15 minutes in a 350° oven. Add cream and bake for five more minutes.

VEAL SAVOYARDE   *Serves 4*

8 3-ounce scallops of veal
¼ cup oil
8 thin slices of Gruyère cheese
8 slices of ham, thinly sliced (such as Cure 81)
1 pint cream
½ cup white wine
2 ounces butter
Paprika
Juice of ½ lemon

Veal dishes lend themselves to a full-bodied French white Burgundy, a California Chardonnay, or a light Italian Red wine, such as a Bardolino, or a Merlot.

Sauté veal in hot oil, turning once. Place a slice of ham and a slice of cheese on top of each. Sprinkle with a little paprika and put the pan in a 350° oven for 5 minutes to melt the cheese. Then put the meat on plates and keep warm. Deglaze the pan with white wine and lemon. Reduce liquid to a syrup consistency, add cream and reduce again to ⅓ of its volume. Add butter. Pour over the meat and serve at once.

SEAFOOD CURRY

Serves 4

4 ounces shrimp or lobster (large shrimp)
1 cup crabmeat
5 ounces Bay shrimp
1 cup sea scallops
Butter for sautéing

To Make the Sauce:
¼ banana
¼ apple
1 stalk of celery
½ carrot, chopped
¼ onion, chopped
1 quart chicken broth
1 tablespoon curry powder
Salt, pepper
2 ounces butter
3 ounces heavy cream

Serve with a Gewürztraminer from Alsace or from California.

Sauté the onions, banana, apple, celery and carrot. Add the curry, chicken broth, salt and pepper. Cook for 15 minutes. Pour in a blender to make it smooth, then strain it through a sieve. Return sauce to low heat. Add cream and check the seasoning. Sauté seafood in butter and add to the sauce. Do not cook after adding it.

TENDERLOIN OF BEEF EN CROÛTE

Serves 4

2 pounds beef tenderloin, cut in large dice
1 pound of mushrooms, quartered and sautéed in butter
2 carrots, cut in julienne strips
½ onion, sliced
2 garlic cloves, minced
1½ ounces flour
3 cups red wine
2 cups veal stock
Bay leaves, thyme, rosemary, salt and pepper

Avocado Seafood Salad

Tenderloin en Croûte

Sauté the beef with onions and carrot strips in butter. When brown, add the garlic, herbs, salt, pepper and flour. Stir well and add red wine. Let it reduce ½. Pour in veal stock and the sautéed mushrooms. Cook for 45 minutes over low heat. Divide into four portions in cocotte dishes. Cover each with a crust of puff pastry cut to fit (See Puff Paste recipe in Pastry Section). Bake for ten minutes in a 375° oven.

Select the red wine of your choice for this beef dish.

***

Occasionally, an inspiration in the Grille produces a special beverage, such as French/Italian Riviera. Perform this cozy after-dinner drink ritual at the table. It has too much class to be kept in the kitchen, and it's too much fun to be kept secret. Caution: Do not sniff and sip simultaneously.

FRENCH/ITALIAN RIVIERA

For the French version, use 1 ounce of Grand Marnier and for the Italian, use Saronno Amaretto. For either, you will need a small splash of Remy Martin or Courvoisier, to offset the sweetness with a hint of cognac flavor, and ¼ slice of orange. Heat a small metal pitcher and a brandy snifter with boiling water, as you would a teapot. Discard the water in each. Pour the Grand Marnier or Amaretto in the pitcher, add the dash of cognac, and swirl briefly. Press ¼ slice of orange into the snifter with a fork, mashing it slightly, and pour the drink mixture over it.

INTERNATIONAL SPY COFFEE

This drink transports you to five countries in just one ounce, according to inventors Gary Hensarling and Barry Crowder. Make it exactly right with a calibrated dropper, if you seek perfection. Into each cup, drop (or splash) ¼ ounce of each: *B&B, Kahlua, Grand Marnier, Jameson's Irish Whiskey,* and

Amaretto. Add the hot coffee (either *Stewart's* or your own kind), a dollop of whipped cream, and one coffee bean on top (the Private Eye).

The Palm Bar

Entered from the sidewalk revolving-door, the Palm Bar has become a lunchtime favorite with business people and shoppers as well as patrons of the hotel. The atmosphere is informal. The food is light, but substantial.

The *French Onion Soup* is available every day, but the spoken menu always offers another soup du jour. Standard menu items include the *Croissant Sandwich* (with turkey, beef or ham). The croissants come from the hotel pastry kitchen, of course. The *Supreme Salad* (chicken salad accompanied by raw vegetables) and the *Chef Salad* are both very large, enough for friends to share, and absolutely fresh. The seafood specialty is a basket of clams, or sometimes shrimp, steamed in white wine.

The special sandwich inventions are worth investigating. Here are some unusual combinations.

L' EXTRAVAGANCE   *Serves 1*

Wheat and pumpernickel breads, one slice of each
3 ounces fresh crabmeat
1 ounce baby Bay shrimp
1 tablespoon bourbon
¼ cup radish sprouts (similar to alfalfa, but tastier)
2 slices smoked salmon
¼ cup Louis Dressing (see Dressings section)
1 teaspoon fresh lemon juice

Mix together crabmeat, shrimp, bourbon, dressing and lemon juice. Using the pumpernickel bread for a base, cover with a slice of smoked salmon. Cover with half the radish sprouts, then the crab and shrimp mixture, more radish sprouts, another slice of smoked salmon and the whole wheat slice.

POULET à la VODKA en CROISSANT

3 Double or
6 Small Servings

6 small croissants
1 pound sliced mushrooms, sautéed in butter and lifted out
3 ounces vodka
Juice of ½ lemon
1 pint mayonnaise
3 ounces sour cream
1 pound diced, cooked chicken
¼ cup onion, diced
Salt and pepper
2 ounces alfalfa sprouts

Split croissants. Put 1/6 of the alfalfa sprouts on each lower half. Mix all other ingredients and spread over alfalfa sprouts. Cover with croissant tops.

SANDWICH à L'ENVERS (INSIDE-OUT SANDWICH)

Serves 1

2 slices Gruyère cheese
2 leaves iceberg lettuce
2 thick slices of tomato
2 ounces sliced, baked turkey
2 ounces of sliced ham
1 croissant, split

Put one slice of Gruyère on the plate as a base. Stack half the lettuce and tomato, all of the turkey, then the split croissant opened flat. Follow with all the ham, the rest of the tomato and lettuce and top with the remaining slice of cheese. Serve with Thousand Island or mayonnaise. Of course, it must be eaten with a knife and fork.

The following sandwiches are served warm.

LE DELI   *Serves 2*

> *1 onion roll*
> *1 rye roll*
> *3 ounces peppered beef*
> *4 ounces pastrami*
> *3 ounces corned beef*
> *3 ounces shredded lettuce*
> *4 slices Provolone*
> *2 slices tomato*

Slice each roll in half. On the bottom half of each, place half
the lettuce, pastrami, peppered beef, corned beef, two slices of
Provolone, tomato and cover, switching the tops of the two
rolls. Heat in a microwave, just until the cheese melts. Then
cut each sandwich in two, switching halves to serve one half
with the rye on top and one, with the onion on top.

SANDWICH TROUVAILLE GREC   *Serves 1*

> *1 small pita bread loaf*
> *3 ounces chopped, cooked lamb*
> *1 egg*
> *2 thin slices of tomato*
> *2 ounces shredded lettuce*
> *1 ounce sour cream*
> *¼ avocado, sprinkled with 1 teaspoon lemon juice*

Make an incision in the thin edge of the pita loaf. Holding the
loaf in a vertical position, drop in half of the lettuce and insert
the meat. Break open the egg and drop it in, raw. Add the rest
of the lettuce, tomatoes, sour cream and the avocado. Stand the
loaf on edge in a microwave-cooking container. Bake one
minute.

CHEF SALAD

1 large salad

Four large lettuce leaves (leaf lettuce)
½ head iceberg lettuce, cut bite-size
1½ ounces beef julienne strips
1½ ounces ham julienne strips
1½ ounces turkey julienne strips
1½ ounces Swiss cheese
2 slices red onion
2 slices tomato
2 black olives
3 spears white asparagus, cooked
¼ cup red cabbage, shredded
¼ cup alfalfa sprouts
3 wedges of hard-boiled egg
3 wedges of tomatoes

Arrange lettuce leaves on the bottom of a glass bowl, filling the center with iceberg lettuce. Arrange the beef, turkey, ham, cheese, asparagus spears, wedges of tomato and wedges of hard-boiled egg on top of the lettuce. Put the red cabbage and alfalfa sprouts in the center, with an olive on each side. Place tomato and red onion to one side. Serve with your choice of dressing.

SUPREME SALAD

Serves 4

2 tomatoes
4 chicken breasts, cooked in water or broth
1 branch of celery, chopped
1 julienne-cut carrot
1 zucchini, julienne cut
1 small red cabbage, shredded
2 ounces alfalfa sprouts
1 head iceberg lettuce, diced for a salad bowl
1 cup mayonnaise
Salt and pepper, if desired

Cut chicken into large dice and mix with chopped celery and mayonnaise. Divide the lettuce into four bowls. Mound chicken-mayonnaise mixture in the center of each. Arrange the carrot, zucchini and cabbage around the chicken. Place the alfalfa on one side and two quarters of tomato on the other.

STEAMED VEGETABLES WITH HERBED BUTTER

Serves 1

For Each Serving:
1 sliced carrot
1 sliced zucchini
2 clusters cauliflower
2 clusters broccoli
2 pieces yellow squash
1 ring of red bell pepper

Steam all but bell pepper for 10 minutes. Vegetables should be crisp. Before serving, steam again for 7 minutes and serve with bell pepper ring on top, and a large pat of the following herbed butter.

Use either fresh or dried herbs to make:

Herbed Butter

1 pound butter
2 tablespoons fresh thyme (1 tablespoon dried)
2 tablespoons fresh rosemary (1 tablespoon dried)
1 teaspoon fresh tarragon leaves (½ teaspoon dried)
1 or 2 bay leaves, crushed
1 teaspoon basil
1 clove garlic, crushed
2 shallots
⅓ cup fresh parsley
1 cup white wine
Salt and pepper to taste

Chop herbs very finely. Soften butter to room temperature. Mix butter with everything, adding the salt, pepper and wine at the last. Roll in aluminum foil to make a loaf and store in the refrigerator.

BASKET OF STEAMED CLAMS

Serves 4

4 pounds fresh, Littleneck clams
1 cup white wine
1 tablespoon chopped parsley
1 chopped onion

A carafe of Chablis or other table white wine will go well with steamed seafoods or vegetables.

Put clams in a steamer, or a large pot with a stainless tray, and allow them to steam in the wine, parsley and onions. Allow to steam for 8-10 minutes. Serve in individual baskets or soup bowls.

This New England-style clam chowder is the specialty of Ed Hubbard, who makes all the soups for the Adolphus restaurants, not only those featured in this recipe collection, but every *soup du jour*. This chowder is also served in the Grille and is very popular in both restaurants.

CLAM CHOWDER

About 6 cups

2 tablespoons butter
1 medium onion
1 green bell pepper
1 stalk celery
1 carrot
1 pinch thyme
2 tablespoons flour
1 quart clam juice
1 large potato, pared and diced
1 bay leaf
1 cup chopped clams
1 cup heavy cream
Pinches of salt and black pepper to taste
¼ cup butter
1 tablespoon fresh, chopped parsley

Dice the onion, green pepper, celery and carrot. Sauté in butter with a pinch of thyme added. Dust with 2 tablespoons flour to absorb moisture. Add the clam juice, potato, and bay leaf. Simmer for ten minutes, or until vegetables are tender. Add 1 cup chopped clams and simmer for no more than 5 minutes. Add 1 cup heavy cream, salt and pepper. Stir in the solid butter and the chopped parsley. Serve hot.

BAKED ONION SOUP   *Serves 8*

4 sliced onions
2 ounces butter
4 ounces white wine
2 quarts chicken stock
Mignonette black pepper (coarsely ground)
Salt to taste
Bouquet garni: *thyme, bay leaves, oregano and parsley*
2 ounces Port wine
2 egg yolks
Grated Gruyère and Parmesan cheese

Melt butter in a large pan, add onions and brown lightly over low heat. Add white wine, chicken stock, spices and *bouquet garni* and let simmer for 30 minutes. Pour into soup cups or bowls, with a round of toasted French bread on top. Sprinkle heavily with Gruyère and Parmesan cheese. Mix the Port wine with the egg yolks and pour over each serving. Brown under broiler, flame and serve.

If serving for a buffet, or in any large quantity, leave out the Port and egg yolks. Simply melt cheese under broiler.

Drinks

A number of extraordinary beverages presented in the various Adolphus bars merit inclusion in this recipe collection. Space limitations permit mention of a mere half-dozen cold drinks and only two hot ones (*see Grille section*).

DALLAS TAXES *(TAXES, NOT TEXAS)*

1½ ounces Cuervo Gold
1 ounce Amaretto
½ ounce Southern Comfort
1½ ounces sweet and sour mix
2 drops champagne

Margaritas in fancy dress — a colorful party starter

Shake, pour over ice. Serve in a wine glass with a salt rim, garnished with a ripe strawberry and a crisp, green Dollar Bill fan.

MIDORI COLADA

1½ ounces Midori
½ ounce rum
½ ounce light cacao
2 ounces Coco Lopez
3 ounces pineapple juice
2 ounces sliced pineapple

Blend and serve in a wine glass, garnished with a pineapple flag.

FROZEN STRAWBERRY CHAMPAGNE

3 ounces fresh strawberries
4 ounces champagne
1 ounce Frais du Bois Strawberry Liqueur
Chipped ice

Pour ingredients and ice into blender. Mix quickly and serve in a champagne or wine glass, garnished with a large strawberry.

KATRINKA

1 ounce vodka
½ ounce Apry
1½ ounces apricot nectar
1½ ounces sweet and sour mix

Shake, pour over ice. Serve in a wine glass, garnished with an apricot flag.

FRESH PEACH DAIQUIRI

A fresh fruit drink
for summer
entertaining —
frosty cold, but not
too sweet

3 ounces fresh peaches
1½ ounces rum
Small scoop of vanilla ice cream
Chipped ice

Blend all together quickly in blender and serve in a wine glass, or a tulip glass, garnished with a slice of fresh peach.

LYNCHBERG LEMONADE

1 ounce Jack Daniels
¾ ounce triple sec
1½ ounces sweet and sour mix
7-Up to top

Serve over ice in a highball glass, garnished with a lemon wedge.

Stocks, Dressings and Sauces

CHICKEN STOCK

For simple stock, the important ingredient is bones, not meat. For use in making soups of all kinds, have simple stock on hand. Notice that it has no salt. Salt should be added according to the soup recipe.

3 pounds chicken bones
1 carrot
1 leek
1 celery branch
1 bouquet garni (thyme, parsley, oregano, bay leaves)
2 gallons water

Blanch chicken bones by bringing water to a boil. Strain off water and replace with enough water to cover the bones. Add the carrot, leek, celery and *bouquet garni*. Cook from four to six hours over low heat. Cool stock and strain before storing in the refrigerator. Keeps 7-10 days.

FISH STOCK

3 pounds fresh fish bones and trimmings (sole, halibut or whitefish)
½ gallon water
1 cup white wine
6 peppercorns
½ teaspoon salt
1 minced onion
1 bunch of parsley
1 minced leek
Juice of 1 lemon
3 ounces mushrooms
2 ounces butter

Sauté the onions, leek, parsley and mushrooms in the butter. Add the fish bones and lemon juice. Cover and cook slowly for

5-10 minutes, stirring at intervals to keep from sticking. Add the white wine and reduce the liquid to about half. Add water and bring the mixture to a boil. Skim the top carefully, then cook gently for 30 minutes on very low heat. Strain through a fine mesh, cool the stock, and store it in the refrigerator until needed.

BROWN VEAL STOCK (ESPAGNOLE)

3 pounds veal bones and trimmings
6 quarts plus 1 pint chicken stock

Mirepoix: *1 onion, 1 carrot, 1 celery stick*
1 bag with mixed herbs: 1 bay leaf, with ¼ teaspoon
  each of thyme, rosemary, parsley
7 ounces tomato paste

Brown the partly broken bones with a little fat in the oven. Add tomato paste and the *mirepoix* and roast a little longer. Pour off the fat, place bones and juice in a big pot on the range. Add chicken stock and herbs. Simmer for six to eight hours, skimming the top frequently. Press through a fine strainer and stir with a wooden spoon until cool. This stock is used for the Demi-glaze for *Petite Fricassée Provençale* and other dishes.

DEMI-GLAZE

Reduce the Brown Veal Stock to half. Add 1 cup Madeira and ¼ cup sautéed whole mushrooms. Salt and pepper to taste.

LOUIS DRESSING

1 cup mayonnaise
½ cup catsup
1 tablespoon cognac
1 teaspoon lemon juice
Salt and pepper

Begin with mayonnaise and add other ingredients while beating with a whisk.

RUSSIAN DRESSING

3 ounces mayonnaise
1½ ounce catsup
1 chopped, hardboiled egg
½ sour pickle, chopped
2 or 3 drops Worcestershire
Salt and pepper

Begin with mayonnaise and add other ingredients while beating with a whisk.

ROQUEFORT DRESSING

2 ounces Roquefort cheese
2 ounces mayonnaise
1 ounce buttermilk
2 ounces sour cream
¼ cup lemon juice
2 or 3 drops Worcestershire
½ tablespoon chopped parsley

Begin with mayonnaise and add other ingredients while beating with a whisk.

VINAIGRETTE DRESSING

2 ounces Dijon mustard
1 egg yolk
2 ounces red wine vinegar
½ ounce chopped shallots
6 ounces salad oil
Salt and pepper

Begin by beating egg yolk with a whisk. Add mustard. Add oil in a slow drizzle while continuing to beat. Add vinegar and salt and pepper to taste.

French sauces are made by boiling down liquid ingredients to a thicker concentration and stronger flavor, then adding other ingredients and sometimes reducing them again. No *saucier* can tell you exactly how long a reduction takes, nor give the exact amount of seasoning. The sauce simply looks, feels and tastes right. Start with small bits of the indicated ingredients and add more if necessary. Taste the sauce to adjust seasoning. Once it suits you, write down the measurement.

BORDELAISE SAUCE

Makes 1 Quart

2 chopped shallots
2 tablespoons butter
2 cups red wine
1 quart Demi-glaze
Cracked black pepper
Thyme, bay leaf, salt

Sauté shallots in one tablespoon butter until soft and yellow. Add herbs and pepper. Deglaze with red wine. Reduce to the consistency of syrup, about two tablespoons of liquid. Add Demi-glaze and reduce to ⅔ of the volume. Finish by adding the rest of the butter and salt. Recipe may be halved.

ROUENNAISE SAUCE

Makes 1 Quart

Follow the recipe for Bordelaise Sauce, but add 1 finely chopped duck liver. Do not allow mixture to boil. Strain through cheesecloth and add a bit more pepper than the Bordelaise Sauce requires. If you want a thicker sauce, add 1 cup Madeira after the first reduction and reduce again. Serve with duck, quail, squab and pheasant. Recipe may be halved.

FISH SAUCE

Makes 1 Quart

2 cups dry white wine
1 quart fish stock
1 pint cream, heavy
3 shallots, chopped
1 ounce mushrooms, chopped
¼ cup butter
Salt, pepper and bay leaves

Sauté shallots with 2 tablespoons butter. Do not brown. Add mushrooms and wine and reduce to 2 tablespoons. Add fish stock and reduce ⅓, then add cream, and reduce ⅓ again. Finish with seasoning and remaining butter. Strain the sauce.

SAUCE PROVENÇALE

Makes 2 Cups

5 tomatoes, peeled, seeded, chopped
2 tablespoons olive oil
3 cloves garlic
½ chopped onion
1 teaspoon chopped parsley
Salt and pepper to taste
Bay leaves, thyme, rosemary and oregano to season

Sauté onion in olive oil. Add garlic, tomatoes, herbs and seasoning. Cook 20 minutes over low heat.

BÉCHAMEL SAUCE

Makes 1 Quart

1 quart milk, scalded
⅓ cup flour
⅓ cup butter
Salt, pepper, nutmeg

Make a *roux* of the butter and flour. Stir to cook, but do not brown. Add the hot milk and cook, stirring constantly until smooth and thick. If the sauce becomes too thick, add more milk. Season and strain. Recipe may be halved.

NANTUA SAUCE

1 pound whole crayfish
¼ cup butter
3 shallots, chopped
¼ cup onions, chopped
½ cup carrots, chopped
1 tablespoon tomato paste
1 clove garlic, minced
1 teaspoon black pepper, cracked
1 bunch fresh tarragon
4 ounces brandy
1½ cups white wine
1 pint fish stock
1½ quarts whipping cream

Sauté crayfish in ¼ cup butter. Add shallots, onion and carrots, tomato paste, garlic, fresh pepper and tarragon. Flambé with brandy and reduce almost dry. Add white wine and fish stock. Reduce by ⅔ and add cream. Cook over low flame. Season with salt and pepper. When the mixture reaches a syrup consistency, strain sauce through a large strainer, pressing it through to extract the full flavor. Recipe may be halved. This sauce recipe may be used for Cream Lobster Sauce, with the substitution of lobster for crayfish.

HOLLANDAISE SAUCE

2 egg yolks
1 tablespoon water
1 tablespoon lemon juice
Salt and white pepper
Cayenne, if desired
¾ cup clarified butter, warm

Beat egg yolks and water in top of double boiler until thick, but not solid. Add butter slowly in a fine stream while beating with a whisk. Stir in lemon juice and season with salt and pepper.

BÉARNAISE SAUCE   *Makes 2½ Cups*

2 cups Hollandaise sauce
2 chopped shallots
2 tablespoons fresh tarragon
Pinch of thyme, chervil and 1 bay leaf
¼ cup white vinegar
¼ cup white wine
Salt and pepper

Mix shallots, herbs, vinegar and white wine in saucepan.
Reduce by ⅔ and set aside to cool. Add to Hollandaise and correct the seasoning, if necessary.

PÉRIGUEUX SAUCE   *Makes 1 Quart*

2 cups Madeira
2 ounces truffle juice
½ ounce truffle peeling
1 quart Demi-glaze
1 small shallot, chopped
2 tablespoons butter

Sauté shallot in 1 tablespoon of butter. Add Madeira and cook
to reduce to 2 tablespoons. Add Demi-glaze and truffle juice.
Reduce to ⅔ the volume. Strain reduction and finish by adding
remaining butter, truffle peeling and seasoning. Recipe may
be halved.
Note: To make Périgourdine, follow the same recipe, but add
1½ ounces canned duck liver pâté.

MUSTARD SEED SAUCE   *Makes 1 Quart*

2 large shallots, chopped
2 cups dry white wine
1 quart heavy cream
1 ounce Demi-glaze made with chicken stock
1 ounce butter
2 ounces mustard seed (¼ cup)
Salt and pepper to taste

The Palm Bar

Sauté the shallots in butter, add white wine and reduce until almost dry. Add heavy cream and reduce by ½. Add Demi-glaze and bring to a boil. Add butter and mustard seed. Mix in blender. Season with salt and white pepper.

This sauce may be made with 2 tablespoons Dijon mustard instead of mustard seed.

Afternoon Tea

When Afternoon Tea in the Lobby begins at the Adolphus, first time celebrants can hardly believe their eyes and taste buds. The setting is elegant and the tea ritual has a distinctly continental flavor. Tea is served from Bavarian china, set on small tables within furniture groupings, accompanied by soft music from the dark, ornate Steinway grand piano.

The tea cart itself offers a choice of at least ten kinds of tea. Once a selection is made and the tea is steeping in the china pot, the Parisian pastry cart steals the show.

In addition to four kinds of dainty sandwiches, the cart holds an incredible array of cakes, tarts, pastries, cookies and truffles. The recipes in this section represent some of the favorites from Afternoon Tea. The selection changes frequently, but these favorites appear almost daily.

LEMON TART   *Serves 12-15*

> 1 10″ sugar shell, baked, or 12 small shells
> 5 medium whole eggs
> 2 egg yolks
> 3 medium lemons and their zest (grated peel, yellow only)
> 1 cup granulated sugar
> ⅓ pound unsalted butter, softened

Lemon or Fruit Tarts will go nicely with a French Sauternes or Monbazillac.

To avoid metallic taste, clean the upper part of an aluminum or stainless steel double boiler with ½ lemon and 2 tablespoons salt before beginning. Scrub the salt around with the cut side of the lemon until the salt appears dirty and the pan is shiny clean. Rinse.

Cook the eggs, extra yolks, juice of three lemons, the lemon zest and the sugar over hot, not boiling water. Beat constantly with a soft whisk for 5 minutes, until mixture doubles in size and will coat a metal spoon. The mixture will seem light and creamy. Add the soft, unmelted butter slowly, mixing 2 or 3 minutes more with the whisk. Pour all into a baked Sweet

Afternoon Tea

Pastry shell and bake in a pre-heated 475° oven for 2 minutes. WATCH IT. Custard should just set. Cool at least three hours. Brush with Apricot Glaze *(see Pastry Kitchen section)* and decorate with thin, dainty lime or lemon triangles and raspberries or strawberries if desired.

Tiny, soft macaroons on the Afternoon Tea cart make a good addition to your own tea tray. The only challenge lies in finding either almond flour or almond meal in a specialty shop or a health food store. This recipe makes 72 small cookies which, when joined in pairs with raspberry jam, tallies three dozen.

SOFT MACAROONS   *3 dozen*

1 cup almond meal or almond flour (sift before measuring)
3 egg whites, whipped with 1 tablespoon granulated sugar
1½ cups powdered sugar

Sift powdered sugar with almond flour. Whip egg whites with granulated sugar till stiff, but not dry. Immediately, fold dry mixture into egg white mixture. Drop by teaspoonfuls onto a paper-lined baking sheet. Bake 10-12 minutes at 375° until light brown. Do not try to remove from paper until completely cooled. Stick two together with raspberry or apricot jam, melted semi-sweet chocolate, or orange marmalade.

ALMOND TUILES   *6 dozen*

½ cup butter, melted and slightly browned
5 medium egg whites
1¼ cups granulated sugar
2 cups sliced almonds, with skins
1 cup flour, sifted

Preheat oven to 350°. For curving the cookies, prepare a long, U-shaped mold of heavy aluminum foil by folding over the sheet of foil four times to make a flat strip measuring 10″ x 3″. Curve the long sides upward so the strip resembles a long trough. Stir butter over direct heat until it becomes slightly browned. Beat egg whites slightly with a wire whisk. Continue whisking as sugar and almonds are added. Add flour and melted butter, stirring to mix. Drop level teaspoonfuls of batter onto a greased baking sheet, flattening each cookie with the back of a spoon. Bake only about 8 cookies at a time, for 7 or 8 minutes. They will be light brown around the edges. Remove immediately from sheet and drop each cookie, while still soft, briefly into the mold. They should still be soft enough to curve without breaking.

SCONES   *1½ dozen*

The texture of these scones begins with mixing the old-fashioned way.

2 cups sifted bread flour
2 cups sifted cake flour
2 tablespoons, plus 2 teaspoons baking powder
1 teaspoon salt
1 tablespoon sugar
1 cup vegetable shortening
1 cup milk
1 cup sour cream
2 cups raisins
Beaten egg to brush tops

Place dry ingredients into a mixing bowl with shortening, and blend with fingers, rather than electric mixer. Mix the milk and sour cream in a separate bowl. Combine the two mixtures until dry ingredients are moistened. Do not overmix. Add the raisins. Sprinkle flour on the work surface to keep the dough from sticking. Pat out dough with hands, not a rolling pin, to ¾ inches. Cut into 2½ inch rounds with a biscuit cutter. Place close together, but not touching, on a baking sheet lined with plain paper. Bake 10 minutes at 425°, then lower the oven heat to 375°. Set another baking sheet below the first one, at this point, to keep the bottom from becoming too brown. Bake 10 more minutes. Remove from oven and serve as soon as possible.

Assorted Delights from the Pastry Kitchen

POUND CAKE

2 medium loaves

With the rich pound cake desserts offer a Vin Cremant Mousseux or after-dinner coffee.

1 pound unsalted butter
3½ cups sifted powdered sugar
8 eggs, medium, at room temperature
3½ cups sifted all-purpose flour
1 tablespoon baking powder
½ cup milk
2 tablespoons vanilla

Mix butter and powdered sugar for 3 minutes at medium speed. Add eggs one at a time, mixing after each one. After all eggs are added, mix another 2 minutes. Sift baking powder and flour together and add alternately with milk, beginning and ending with flour. Mix 3 minutes, or until smooth. Add vanilla. Bake in 2 greased 5 x 7 loaf pans. Begin at 375° for 10 minutes, then lower oven to 350° about 40 minutes. Test with a toothpick for doneness.

To Make Fruit Cakes: Using the same mixture and method, fold in at the last: 2 cups mixed fruit (*Hero,* if possible), 2 cups raisins, 1 cup glazed red cherries, zest of 1 lemon and of 1 orange, 2 tablespoons cinnamon, ¼ cup dark rum or brandy. Bake the same as above, but about 10 minutes longer. *Makes 3 loaves.*

ALMOND OR PECAN COOKIES

Makes 2 9" pans

1 cup plus 1 tablespoon granulated sugar
½ cup honey
¼ pound butter
⅓ cup cream, room temperature
3½ cups sliced almonds or pecans
1 pound of sugar paste (see Pastry section)

Press paste into greased pans, bringing it a fraction of an inch up the side, just enough to keep the filling from running below the crust. Bake for 5 minutes at 375°. Allow to cool for ten minutes. Meanwhile, mix sugar, honey and butter. Cook over medium heat until golden caramel color, about 6 minutes. Remove from heat and add cream and almonds. Spread the mixture over the crust and cook at 375° for 5 minutes, just until golden brown. Allow the pan to cool, then cut into strips or squares.

FRUIT TARTS

Refer to *Pastry Kitchen* section recipes for *Sweet Pastry*, *Pastry Cream* and *Apricot Glaze*. Fill tart shells with the cream, cover with sliced strawberries, kiwi fruit or raspberries and glaze. Top with whipped cream, if desired.

STRAWBERRY NAPOLEONS   *8 slices*

1 pound puff paste (see Pastry section)
1¾ cups pastry cream
1 pint fresh strawberries
1½ cups unsweetened cream, whipped
¼ cup powdered sugar

Roll out pastry 3/16″ thick in a rectangle to fit a 12″ x 16″ baking pan lined with plain white paper. Bake at 400° for 10 minutes. Invert pastry onto back side of another baking pan covered with the same kind of paper. Bake ten more minutes at 400°. Cool, and cut into three long strips, sixteen by four inches each. Wash and dry berries. Slice about ¼″ thick. Spread first strip with 1 cup pastry cream. Cover with a generous layer of berries all facing the same direction. Press them into the filling. Spread ¾ cup whipped cream over the berries. Place second pastry layer over the cream. Layer remaining pastry cream and berries. Spread with whipped cream, reserving just about ⅛ cup to use for frosting the sides. Place remaining layer of pastry on top. Smooth whipped cream around the sides and sprinkle powdered sugar over the top. Slice into 2″ slices. Note: The bottom layer should have slightly more filling than the top for the best appearing Napoleon slices.

Serve Strawberry Napoleons with a Demi-sec Perrier Joet.

Decorated Cheesecakes
(inset) Strawberry and Kiwi Tarts with Strawberry Napoleon

PALAIS RAISINS

5 dozen

⅓ pound butter (¾ cup)
¾ cup granulated sugar
3 eggs
1¼ cups raisins
1⅓ cups flour
1 tablespoon rum (optional)

Mix butter and sugar for two minutes until smooth. Add whole eggs one at a time. Mix two more minutes. Add ⅓ cup of flour to the raisins and chop coarsely. Add raisins and remaining flour to mixture in bowl. Add rum and mix one minute or less. Drop by tablespoonfuls onto a baking sheet lined with plain white paper. Bake at 375° for 17 minutes, or until edges are slightly brown. Allow to cool before removing from pan. Keep dry and covered.

CROQUET SUISSE

6-7 dozen

½ pound plus 1 tablespoon butter
1¾ cups powdered sugar
3 cups all-purpose flour, sifted
3 cups pecan pieces
2 egg whites, large, unbeaten
1 teaspoon cinnamon

Allow butter to soften to room temperature and mix with powdered sugar until smooth. Add flour and mix until flour disappears. Mix the pecans with unbeaten egg whites and fold into mixture. Then stir in cinnamon (do not overbeat). Form into a square, 8" x ¾" thick. Wrap in plastic and freeze until firm. Remove dough from freezer and defrost only slightly before cutting. Divide into four strips, slicing each strip into ¼" cookies. Lay the cookies flat on a lightly greased baking sheet and bake at 375° for 10-12 minutes. Unbaked dough will stay fresh in freezer about four weeks.

One of the most inviting treats on the pastry cart is the soft pastel assortment of petits fours. They can be cut into any desired shape, frosted any color and decorated your own way. Basically, you need thin layers of cake, simple syrup, jam or other filling, and fondant glaze. The same fondant glaze can be used over tiny eclairs or puffs, filled with pastry cream. The choux petits fours also appear on the pastry cart.

PETITS FOURS

4 dozen

½ cup plus 1 tablespoon butter
1¼ cups granulated sugar
1 teaspoon vanilla
2 cups sifted, all-purpose flour
1 tablespoon baking powder
½ teaspoon salt
¾ cup milk
3 eggs

To Make Cake: Preheat oven to 375°. Butter a 9″ x 13″ baking pan. Cream softened butter and sugar in a large bowl until light and fluffy. Add vanilla and mix at medium speed 2 minutes. Sift together flour, salt and baking powder. Add to butter mixture alternately with milk in two or three portions, beginning and ending with flour. Beat at medium speed for 2 minutes, scraping sides of bowl. Add eggs and beat 2 more minutes. Pour into baking pan and bake 25-30 minutes until firm to the touch. Cool cake in the pan 15 minutes and turn out on wax paper.

Why not sip a glass of Champagne or a California sparkling wine with these?

To Make Fondant Glaze: Place 3 cups of confectioners sugar in a large pan. Over low heat, gradually add ¼ cup of water, stirring with a wire whisk to a smooth paste. Add another tablespoonful, a few drops at a time, if necessary, and continue to stir until consistency of thin corn syrup. Add soft color, if desired, or ¼ cup melted, semi-sweet chocolate.

To Assemble: When cold, split cake into 2 9″ x 13″ layers and brush the top of each with simple syrup. (Make simple syrup by bringing to a boil 1 cup sugar and 1 cup water. Flavor the mixture with 1 tablespoon rum.) Spread jam or filling on one layer and cover with the second. Cut cake into dainty squares (about 1½ inches). Set squares 2 inches apart on a rack over a baking sheet. Spoon or pour hot glaze over cakes to form a thin, almost transparent coating. Decorate with fruit, candies or crystallized violets, and Butter Cream icing.

CREAM PUFF SWANS

To make filled swans, follow *Choux Paste* recipe in *Pastry Kitchen* section, making the recipe to include necks and tails. When puffs are cool, carefully cut tops off with a sharp knife and remove the soft filaments inside. Fill the puffs with Pastry Cream. Cut tops in half and use them to form lifted wings. Using a skewer, carefully punch a small hole in the side of the puff to hold the neck (or place the end just inside the edge of the cream). Place the tails opposite, pointed side down. Sprinkle heavily with powdered sugar. Chill, uncovered, in the refrigerator and store refrigerated.

ECLAIRS

Follow *Choux Paste* recipe. For small puffs or eclairs, force paste through a bag. Large puffs can be dropped from a spoon onto the baking sheet. Spread eclairs into a long shape. Bake and fill with pastry cream. Sprinkle with powdered sugar or frost using any fondant, especially chocolate.

RELIGIEUSE

The stacked Religieuse pastries combine several basic recipes from the pastry kitchen: *Choux Pastry, Pastry Cream, Chocolate Fondant* and *Butter Cream*. The pastry cream is adapted by adding two tablespoons melted, cooled semi-sweet chocolate to 2 cups of (room temperature) pastry cream. Or instead of chocolate, add ½ teaspoon instant coffee dissolved in 1 teaspoon rum. Use 1 medium and 1 small choux puff for each religeuse pastry. Fill each choux shell with pastry cream and glaze with Chocolate Fondant. Stick the smaller puff down onto the larger one with a tiny dab of Butter Cream. Pipe four thin columns of Butter Cream to connect the two puffs.

Chocolate Truffles appear regularly on the pastry cart. The recipe appears in the *Pastry Kitchen* section.

The Pastry Kitchen

Many recipes combine two or more basic pastry products. A number of desserts begin with choux or puff pastry and pastry cream lends itself to many variations. The quickly made apricot glaze brushes easily over several cakes, tarts and Danish rolls. Sweet pastry forms either a base for cheesecake or crust for fruit tart. Fruit tarts are made with sweet pastry, filled with pastry cream, fresh fruit, and covered with an apricot glaze. Each time these basics come up, please refer to this section.

Measurements are adjusted to American standards of cups, spoons, weight and liquid/dry measure. They are in proportion to the original French measure used by the chef. Jean Pierre Piallier, the Chef Patissier, reduced the recipes from very large quantities for this collection, and tested each of them himself to assure the taste and texture remain the same.

Recipes in this section specify unsalted butter, medium eggs and semi-sweet chocolate. Some recipes recommend certain kinds of flour as well. Any substitution may slightly modify the flavor or texture of a dessert.

PASTRY CREAM   *Makes 2 cups*

> 2 cups milk
> 4 egg yolks
> ¾ cup granulated sugar
> 3 tablespoons cornstarch
> 2 tablespoons cake flour
> 1 teaspoon vanilla

Scald milk. Mix egg yolks with sugar until smooth. Add cornstarch and flour and mix slowly. Add half the hot milk to egg mixture, then return all of it to the remaining hot milk. Stir over direct low heat until it boils and thickens. Add vanilla and allow to cool.

To use in Cream Puff Swans, add 2 cups of whipped cream just before filling.

BASIC BUTTER CREAM FROSTING

1⅔ cups granulated sugar
1 cup egg whites
1 pound butter, room temperature
1 cup shortening, room temperature
1 tablespoon vanilla

Warm granulated sugar and egg whites in double boiler until sugar dissolves and they are smooth to the touch. Whip on high setting in electric mixer for eight minutes, or until a spatula cuts a firm path. Change mixer speed to slow and add butter and shortening. Whip again for ten minutes on medium speed until smooth and light. Add vanilla. Butter Cream can be kept up to two weeks in the refrigerator. It makes enough to frost tops of three 9″ layers.

APRICOT GLAZE

5 tablespoons apricot jam
1 tablespoon water
1 teaspoon lemon juice

Bring ingredients to a boil. Cool slightly and spoon or brush over pastry or filling. If it thickens, add a few drops of hot water.

SWEET PASTRY   *12-18 tart shells*

½ pound soft butter
1½ cups granulated sugar
2 eggs
½ teaspoon salt
½ teaspoon baking powder
4 cups all-purpose flour

Soften butter to room temperature, add sugar, and cream with electric mixer. Add whole eggs one at a time and mix well. Sift together flour, salt and baking powder. Add to butter and eggs and mix. Form a ball. Wrap dough in clear plastic and chill in refrigerator 2 hours. This dough may be kept for about one week in the refrigerator, enabling you to use only as much as you wish at one time. Roll out dough ¼-inch thick and cut with a 2-inch round or fluted cutter. Fit into lightly greased muffin tins and bake at 375° for 10-12 minutes, until light golden brown. Cool pastry shells before filling.

PERFECT FILLING   *Makes 2 cups*

> ⅔ *cup pastry cream*
> 1⅓ *cups butter cream*

Have pastry cream at room temperature. Press through a sieve and add flavoring. Use either:

> *1 teaspoon vanilla,*
> ¼ *cup melted, semisweet chocolate, or*
> *1 tablespoon Grand Marnier*

Mix pastry cream and butter cream together until smooth. This combination can be stored in the refrigerator for 3 or 4 days.

Choux Paste lends itself to several desserts when combined with pastry cream or other filling, syrup and whipped cream. The light, buttery shells provide the base for Cream Puffs, Eclairs, Swans and Religieuse.

CHOUX PASTE

> *1 cup boiling water*
> ¼ *pound unsalted butter*
> ¼ *teaspoon salt*
> 1½ *cups flour*
> *6 eggs*

Pour boiling water over butter in a saucepan over heat and stir until butter melts. Add flour all at once and stir with a wooden spoon until the mixture leaves the sides of the pan and forms a ball in the center. Remove from heat. Immediately add unbeaten eggs, one at a time, beating with a wooden spoon to a smooth paste after each addition. Continue beating until mixture is velvet smooth. (If making swans, set aside ⅔ cup of the mixture to make heads and tails). Drop heaping table-spoons of batter onto a greased baking sheet about 3 inches apart. Bake puffs in a pre-heated 400° oven for 15 minutes, or until they are well puffed and delicately browned. Reduce heat to 300° and continue baking puffs 5-10 minutes to allow centers to cook without further browning. Remove from oven and cool.

To Make Swans: Pipe the reserved paste through a large pastry tube, using ⅓-inch round tip, forming a letter "S." Pipe a comma-shaped piece for each tail. Make several extra so you can choose the best ones. Heads and tails should be piped onto a separate greased baking sheet since they require less baking than the puffs. Bake at 350° for 5-10 minutes until light brown.

The cheesecake offered at The Adolphus has many variations, but the four main flavors are lemon, vanilla, almond and chocolate. The same recipe is used for each kind. Be sure to use genuine extracts of lemon, vanilla and almond and real semi-sweet chocolate. The cheesecake will be tall in a 10″ pan (springform, if you have it). Piallier makes 16 at once. This recipe is for one.

CHEESECAKE

2 pounds plus four ounces cream cheese
1⅔ cups granulated sugar, mixed with
½ cup cornstarch
3 extra large eggs
2 cups milk, mixed with
1½ cups sour cream
1 cup dry bread crumbs
Flavoring: Use only one
   2 tablespoons almond essence,
   2 tablespoons lemon extract,
   3 tablespoons vanilla,
   1 cup melted semisweet chocolate

Pre-heat oven to 425°. Press 1 cup dry bread crumbs on the bottom of a well-buttered 10-inch pan. Starting with all ingredients at room temperature, beat softened cream cheese with electric mixer. Mix cream cheese with sugar and cornstarch for three minutes. Add whole eggs, one at a time, mixing after each at medium speed. Mix again for three minutes. Whisk milk and sour cream together and fold into the mixture with a wooden spoon, scraping sides as well until smooth and creamy. Add flavoring. For chocolate flavored cheesecake, fold 1 cup of melted semisweet chocolate into 2 cups of cake batter, then combine with remaining batter. Spoon mixture into the prepared pan.

Some diners enjoy a Port as a counterpoint to this rich cheesecake.

Place cheesecake pan in the center of a large pan of hot water and bake for 50 minutes at 425°, then reduce heat to 375° and bake for 5 minutes. *After the first 25 minutes,* if the top seems to be getting light brown, set a loose sheet of foil over it.

Allow cake to cool completely, at least three hours, before cutting. For best results, refrigerate for one hour before removing from pan. If not using the springform pan, heat the pan briefly on direct heat just long enough to melt the butter cooked into the crumb base. Invert the cake onto a plate or tray, then back to right side up. At the Adolphus, they return the cake right side up onto a sweet pastry crust, but the only purpose is to make a neat serving.

PUFF PASTE   *1 block*

Puff pastry enhances so many dishes that Jean Pierre recommends making two blocks at the same time. Wrapped in plastic or foil, it can be kept in the refrigerator for a week, or in the freezer for three weeks. Freezing puff paste actually improves it.

4 cups (1 pound) bread flour
¼ pound butter, in small pieces
1 teaspoon salt
1¼ cups cold water, preferably ice-cold
¾ pound butter

Sift flour and salt together in a large bowl. Mix in ¼ pound butter with your fingers or a pastry blender as you would for a pie crust. Add water and continue mixing to a thick paste. Form the mass into a ball, cleaning the sides of the bowl. Flatten, cover with plastic wrap, and allow pastry to rest for 20 minutes.

Roll dough out in a circle about one inch thick. Slice ¾ pound butter into uniform slices and fit flat over the dough, leaving a 1½ inch margin. Fold the edge nearest you toward the center, then fold the opposite side to center to touch it. Fold right and left sides over to touch, making the dough a square.

Dust the surface and rolling pin with flour. Roll dough into a rectangle 24 inches long (away from you). Fold into thirds and seal with the rolling pin. Lift the dough and make one quarter of a turn. Roll the dough away from you again to 24" in length and repeat the three-layer fold. Seal with the rolling pin. Punch two fingers into the dough to show the dough has had two single turns. Cover with plastic wrap and refrigerate for 20 minutes.

Repeat the rolling-and-turning twice more. Punch two fingers twice, to show the dough has had four single turns. Cover and refrigerate for 20 more minutes. Remove dough from refrigerator and do the fifth and sixth turns. The dough is ready to use, or may be kept refrigerated or frozen. Before using, roll out dough and cut into desired shapes.

Chocolate

Chocolate recipes appear in the *Pastry Kitchen* section or the *Afternoon Tea* section, but these few special desserts are offered here as outstanding fare for true chocolate aficionados. Take note that Piallier recommends using melted semisweet chocolate in every recipe and little sugar. Traditionally, European-style cakes and desserts are slightly less sweet than their American counterparts.

CHOCOLATE TRUFFLES

Makes 9 dozen

1 pint whipping cream
½ cup granulated sugar
20 ounces semisweet chocolate, melted
8 ounces semisweet chocolate for coating
Cocoa powder for rolling

Bring the cream just to a boil and add sugar. Stir in 20 ounces of chocolate, which has been melted over hot, not boiling, water. When chocolate has dissolved in the cream, it will be thick like a sauce. Cool, then refrigerate covered for one hour or until it is really cold.

Remove chocolate mixture from refrigerator and stir over hot, not boiling, water until it reaches room temperature only. As the mixture loses its chill, it becomes elastic (it should not be heated to a liquid) and can be dropped from a teaspoon in uniform, walnut-size bits on a tray covered with foil or waxed paper. Refrigerate for 30 minutes. Roll in cocoa powder and return them to the refrigerator.

To Coat: Melt remaining semisweet chocolate over hot water. Remove truffles from the refrigerator and dip in melted chocolate to make a shell. Roll in cocoa powder again. These will keep in the refrigerator about two weeks.

CHOCOLATE MOUSSE CAKE WITH MENTHE MERINGUE

(12-15 servings)

Chocolate Sponge:

7 eggs, plus
2 egg yolks (save whites for the meringue)
¾ cup granulated sugar
1 cup flour, unsifted, then sifted three times with
¼ cup cocoa
4 tablespoons unsalted butter, melted and cooled

Heat the eggs and extra yolks with the sugar in a double boiler just to warm, not cook. Then, using a mixer, whip to a froth on high speed and continue for five minutes, then reduce to a medium speed, beating for five more minutes. Add flour and cocoa, slowly folding in by hand with a spatula. Stir in butter. Bake in a well-greased, 10″ x 2½″ round cake pan, (not tube or spring form) for 15 minutes at pre-heated 325°. Then raise the oven temperature to 350° for 15 minutes, or until firm to touch in center. Remove immediately to a cake plate or cardboard circle which has been sprinkled with granulated sugar. Cool for 2 hours; then refrigerate 1 hour before slicing into three layers.

Note: Changes in mixing speeds and oven temperatures are important steps in achieving the right texture (firm, yet fluffy) for easy handling.

Syrup:

¾ cup boiling water
¼ cup granulated sugar
2 tablespoons Kirsch

Add sugar to boiling water. When dissolved, flavor with 2 tablespoons Kirsch and set aside to cool.

Chocolate Mousse Filling:

½ recipe pastry cream
¼ cup melted, cooled semisweet chocolate
3 cups whipping cream

Mix chocolate into pastry cream until smooth; whip cream and fold into the mixture.

To Assemble: Brush each layer with ⅓ of the syrup. Divide the mousse in half and fill between the layers, leaving ½″ margin at the edge. Put the top layer over all, cut side up, and brush with the syrup. Frost with Menthe Meringue.

Menthe Meringue:

4 large egg whites
1 cup sugar
2 tablespoons Crème de Menthe
Few drops of green color

Whisk egg whites and sugar in a double boiler over hot water until sugar is dissolved. Remove from heat and beat at high speed for five minutes or until the meringue stands in peaks. Add Crème de Menthe and a few drops of green (one or two at a time) until the color reaches a soft shade of green. Using a very light hand, ice the cake with the meringue, being sure to cover entirely. Smooth the top and sides, all the way to the plate, and bake at 450° for only three minutes to color lightly toast.

To Decorate: Whip 1 cup of cream and pipe a high rim around the edge of the top layer. Shave curls of semi-sweet chocolate to scatter over the cream and around the sides of the cake. This cake will keep two or three days in the refrigerator . . . if no one knows it's there.

BISCUIT ROULADE

4 whole eggs
3 eggs, separated
¾ cup granulated sugar
¾ cup cake flour, sifted
1 tablespoon granulated sugar

Mix egg yolks, whole eggs and ¾ cup sugar for 10 minutes at medium speed with mixer. Work in cake flour with your hands. In a separate bowl, whip the egg whites and 1 tablespoon sugar to stiff peaks, but not dry. Fold into the flour mixture with a wooden spoon, bringing the spoon over and under until the egg whites disappear. Spread on the back side of a baking sheet covered with plain white paper, leaving a 1" margin. Bake at 425° for 5-8 minutes, or until light brown. When cool, spread with Chocolate Mousse Filling.

Chocolate Mousse Filling

4 egg whites
¾ cup granulated sugar
½ cup melted semisweet chocolate
¼ cup hot water
1 pint whipping cream

Whisk eggs and sugar in a double boiler over low heat and hot water just to warm them and to dissolve sugar. Do not cook.

Whip egg mixture with an electric mixer for 5 minutes at medium speed until stiff. Mix the melted chocolate with hot water until thick. Fold carefully into egg whites with a spatula. Whip cream and fold in. This will keep two days covered in the refrigerator. Spread filling over the biscuit layer and roll like a jelly roll. Frosted with chocolate, it makes a nice Christmas log.

CHOCOLATE MARBLE BIRTHDAY CAKE

½ cup plus 1 tablespoon butter
1¼ cups granulated sugar
2 cups all-purpose flour
1 tablespoon baking powder
½ teaspoon salt
¾ cup milk
3 whole eggs
⅓ cup melted, semisweet chocolate
1 teaspoon almond flavor

Champagne is a nice treat with any of these specialty desserts.

Cream butter with mixer and add sugar. Continue to cream until light and fluffy. Sift flour, measure and resift with baking powder and salt. Add alternately with milk, beginning and ending with flour, in three or four portions. Add whole eggs, beating in one at a time. Remove one cup batter before adding almond flavor to bowl. Stir melted chocolate into reserved cup of batter. Pour light batter into a 10″ well-buttered baking pan. Using a paper funnel or a pastry bag, swirl chocolate mixture in rings, pressing it into the batter as you go.

Bake at 350° for fifteen minutes, then lower the heat to 325° and continue to bake for five to ten more minutes. A table knife inserted in center of cake comes out clean when it is done. Remove from pan after five minutes. Cool on wire rack, then frost.

Chocolate Meringue Icing

5 egg whites
1 cup plus 3 tablespoons granulated sugar
¾ pound butter, softened
½ cup melted semisweet chocolate

Heat egg whites in double boiler with sugar. Beat mixture until sugar is dissolved. Beat on high setting to stiff peaks, then reduce speed to low and beat in butter. Remove two tablespoons for writing on cake, if desired, before adding ½ cup melted chocolate. Beat for 5 minutes on high, until icing is fluffy and smooth.

Chocolate Meringue Icing Variations: One of the following may be substituted for the melted chocolate.

  2 tablespoons powdered, instant coffee dissolved in ¼ cup Kahlua
  2 teaspoons vanilla extract
  1½ teaspoons almond extract

Nouvelle cakes differ from the traditional cakes in that they are made without flour, salt and baking powder, and are served with sauces instead of frostings. Don't be surprised if the cake changes shape slightly or, for that matter, seems to fall in. It's supposed to do that; it won't be heavy. Either of the cakes below can be served with any of the three thin dessert sauces. For thicker sauces, whip ½ cup cream and fold it into the sauce.

NOUVELLE APRICOT CAKE

  12 egg yolks
  ¼ cup granulated sugar for yolks
  1 cup soft butter
  5 egg whites
  ¼ cup granulated sugar
  ½ cup apricot marmalade

Beat egg yolks with ¼ cup granulated sugar for ten minutes until light colored and thick. Add soft butter, mixing well before adding marmalade. Beat egg whites until stiff in a separate bowl, adding ¼ cup sugar and beating until they stand in peaks. Fold into cake mixture. Bake in a well greased 10″ pan, at 250° for 50-55 minutes, until center feels springy to touch. Turn out the cake onto a serving plate immediately and serve with one of the thin dessert sauces below or offer a choice of sauces with whipped cream added to one.

NOUVELLE CHOCOLATE CAKE

12 egg yolks
¼ cup granulated sugar
1½ cups melted semisweet chocolate
½ cup soft butter
5 egg whites
¼ cup granulated sugar

Beat egg yolks with ¼ cup granulated sugar for ten minutes until light colored and thick. Add melted chocolate and soft butter and mix well. Whip egg whites until stiff (using clean beaters and a separate bowl). Add ¼ cup sugar and beat to stiff peaks. Fold into cake mixture and bake at 250° in a well-greased 10″ pan for 50-55 minutes. It should feel firm in the center, but still springy when touched by hand. Turn out immediately. Serve with a dessert sauce.

All three dessert sauces given below compliment either Chocolate or Apricot Nouvelle Cakes.

NOUVELLE DESSERT SAUCES

Orange

Juice of two large oranges
1 tablespoon grated orange zest
½ cup sugar
1 egg
1 cup thick cream

Heat the orange juice with the zest. Mix sugar and egg. Add to juice. When the mixture comes to a boil, add the cream. Whisk over heat until the mixture returns to a boil. Remove immediately and transfer the sauce to a cool bowl.

Vanilla

1 pint milk
5 tablespoons sugar
4 egg yolks
1 teaspoon vanilla
1 or 2 tablespoons honey

Scald milk. Beat egg yolks with sugar. Combine egg yolk mixture with hot milk by adding a small amount of milk to the eggs and sugar, then returning all to the milk pan. Heat over direct flame just until thick enough to coat a metal spoon. Remove immediately from flame. Pour into a cool bowl at once and stir in vanilla and honey.

Chocolate

⅓ cup whipping cream
½ cup melted semisweet chocolate
5 egg yolks
½ cup milk
1 tablespoon honey

Warm the cream, add melted chocolate and beat in egg yolks with a whisk. Bring the milk to a boil and add to the cream mixture by adding a little of the milk, then returning all to the milk pan. Bring just to a boil and remove from pan to a bowl at once. Stir in honey.

Puff Pastries

(See Puff Paste recipe this section)

Puff pastry which has been made in advance and frozen in 1-pound blocks actually turns out better than freshly made paste. It must be thawed in order to be rolled, but the colder it is when put into a hot oven, the lighter and puffier it becomes. Roll it to exact recommended thickness for best results.

BOUCHÉES (Vol-au-Vents)

One pound of puff paste will make 5 large, or 12-15 small cases (2½").

Starting with the paste as cold as possible, roll out to ¼" thickness. Use a 4" cutter to cut out 5. Then mark the center with a smaller cutter (2½") pressing only ⅓ of the way through the paste. Refrigerate at least one hour.

Bake on a plain paper-lined baking sheet, with another sheet of paper, greased, across the tops to make the *bouchées* rise evenly. Bake at 400° for 10 minutes. Reduce over to 350° for 15 minutes. Remove paper and continue baking for five minutes to brown the tops.

PANIER

The elongated puff pastry used for *Petite Fricassée Provençale* (served in The Grille) is called a *Panier*. If the right shape cutter is not available, one can be made by mashing the opening of a 4"-diameter coffee can (one pound) into a 3" x 5" oval. One pound of paste is enough for eight *paniers*.

1 pound puff paste
1 medium egg, beaten

Ideally, roll the paste an even 3/16" thick. Cut into elliptical shape, then stretch each piece slightly. Dip the outer edge of your hand in flour and make an indentation across each *panier* at the three-inch width center. Brush with beaten egg. Using a fork, make criss-cross designs over the top. Place on a baking sheet lined with plain white paper. Place a greased sheet of plain paper across the pastry (any puff pastry thicker than ⅛" needs that). Bake at 400° for 10 minutes, then reduce to 350° for 15 minutes.

Pulled Sugar Basket with Roses

*Nougatine Church with Croque-en-Bouche Fountain
and Assorted French Pastries*

Semi-Sweet Puff Pastries

Palmiers and Bow Ties are made with puff paste which has been rolled out only four times. To make these, you complete turns five and six with ¾ cup of sugar. Sprinkle half of the sugar with each of the last two turns. Roll the pastry out to desired length and sprinkle with an extra ¼ cup sugar. Sprinkle board and rolling pin with granulated sugar.

PALMIERS
Makes 14-16

1 pound block of puff paste

Roll the pastry, as outlined above, to a rectangle 32" x 7" and sprinkle with the last ¼ cup sugar. Bring the short sides (7") to the middle, then bring each side over to the middle again. Then fold one half over the other. The paste is then 3½" x 7". Freeze about 30 minutes before slicing to ½" thickness. Bake *palmiers* on a baking sheet lined with plain white paper two or three inches apart. Slant diagonally on the sheet in alternating rows of three, then two. Bake at 375° for 10 minutes. Turn them to bake their underside 5 minutes. They should be golden brown, with sugar slightly caramelized around the edges. Remember to *sugar* the board and rolling pin, don't use flour on these.

BOW TIES
Makes 16-17
Using 1 pound block

Using the same method as for *palmiers,* roll the paste 6" wide, 10" long and ¾" thick. Shape the edges, trimming with a knife, to make sides straight. Cut into ½" strips each 6" long. Then twist the middle of each and press down the center on a baking sheet lined with plain white paper. Be sure the layered ¾" thick sides are facing upward so the pieces will fan out like bow ties. Bake the same as for the *palmier,* 375° for 10 minutes, then turn to bake the underside 5 minutes.

APPLE TARTS

Makes 6

½ pound puff paste
6 teaspoons Pastry Cream
3 medium sliced apples
Apricot glaze to brush over tarts
Slightly sweetened whipped cream topping, if desired

Core and peel apples. Cut vertically through the center. Remove any remaining seeds and slice in about 12 pieces per half apple. Roll pastry to ⅛" thickness. Cut 3" rounds. Stretch dough slightly, making small rim. Place 1 teaspoon pastry cream in center of each round. Nestle 12 apple slices over pastry cream on each tart. Bake on a baking sheet lined with plain paper for 10 minutes at 400°; then lower over to 350° and bake ten minutes. Brush with apricot glaze after tarts cool. Serve with cream if desired, but they are good without it. The apricot glaze and pastry cream add only a slightly sweet taste.

Tarts and turnovers will often go well with a nice dry sherry.

APPLE TURNOVERS

Makes 5

1 pound puff paste
3 apples, pared and sliced as for tarts, then halved again
⅓ cup sugar
1 teaspoon cinnamon
2 ounces butter
4 drops lemon juice
¼ cup apricot marmalade or jam
Egg wash (1 medium egg beaten, nothing added)

Cook all ingredients together, except the puff paste and the egg, over medium heat for ten minutes. Allow to cool. Roll pastry out to ⅛" thickness. Cut in 6" rounds. Stretch dough slightly and brush egg around outer edge. Place mixture in center, fold, and seal with fingers. Wash the tops twice with egg. Put in oven at 400° for 20 minutes, or until golden brown. After first 15 minutes, slip another baking sheet below the first for double thickness; it keeps the bottom side from becoming too dark.

Assorted Breads

Savories

CHEESE STRAWS

Makes 2 Dozen

½ cup pound puff paste
1 cup grated Parmesan cheese
1½ tablespoons paprika
1 medium egg, beaten, for wash

Roll paste into a rectangle 20″ x 6″. Mark into 19 or 20 strips of one-inch width. Wash with egg, sprinkle with paprika, then spread Parmesan cheese over the whole surface. Cut into strips. Starting at each end, simultaneously twist each strip two or three times and roll lightly with your hands. Lay each strip on *paper-lined* baking sheet, pressing the two ends firmly on the paper. Bake at 400° for 10 minutes. Reduce heat to 350° and bake 5 minutes.

CROISSANTS

Makes 30

These can't be made hurriedly, but they are worth the time and trouble. The paste should be made the day before baking. With some practice, you can learn the skill of rolling and folding them to look their best. High-gluten flour is the secret to making them high and light.

4½ cups high-gluten flour (1 pound 4 ounces)
⅓ cup plus 1 tablespoon granulated sugar

2 ounces butter
¼ cup dry yeast
1½ cups cold milk
¾ pound butter, softened
2 eggs mixed with 1 tablespoon water

The Day Before Baking mix dry ingredients with 2 ounces butter and yeast *(it doesn't have to be dissolved).* Add cold milk and mix at medium speed 5 minutes using the hook attachment to your mixer, or with hands for 10 minutes, until the dough is smooth and elastic. Form into a ball, brush lightly with oil or sprinkle lightly with flour, and cover with plastic wrap. Let rise in a warm place till double in size. It rises only once.

On a floured surface, roll out dough to a rectangle, slightly thicker in the center than on the sides. Place softened butter in center. Fold from both ends, then turn and fold over open ends to make another rectangle 10″ x 15″. Chill 1 hour in the refrigerator.

Roll dough out long. Fold both ends toward center, then one half over the other. Roll out long again and fold one end to the middle and cover with the other end. Sprinkle lightly with flour, wrap in plastic and refrigerate overnight.

Second Day: Roll dough out long, add a little flour for easy handling. Fold ends one over another at the center. Turn dough over and adjust its position to have the folded edges crosswise before you. Roll it out again, away from you, adding flour, to a rectangle 12″ x 36″.

Divide lengthwise into two 6″ strips. Begin triangles by cutting one strip from a corner to four inches from the opposite corner. Then cut across to make a triangle with a four-inch edge on the first side. Continue until you have triangles to make about 30 croissants. To roll up each croissant, stretch it slightly, starting at the big end. Then, roll it over toward you, pressing it slightly, with the two ends brought to a curve to finish the shape.

Place on a baking sheet, either buttered or covered with plain paper. Brush with egg-water mixture. Allow to rise in a warm place (about 90°) for 1½ hours, or until double in size. Bake immediately at 400° 15-18 minutes to a light brown.

QUICHE LORRAINE   *Makes 2 9″ pies*

Piallier makes this classic extra creamy with both sour and heavy cream.

Quiche Pastry

3¾ cups bread flour
2 cups vegetable shortening
2 tablespoons sugar
1 teaspoon salt
¾ cup ice water

Mix dry ingredients and shortening with two knives or a pastry blender. Add ice water 1 tablespoon at a time, tossing with a fork until moist. Cool in refrigerator wrapped in plastic. Roll out and fit into 9" pie tins.

Quiche Filling

1 medium onion, sliced thin
12 ounces smoked ham, in small dice
5 ounces Swiss cheese, grated
2 tablespoons butter

Sauté onions in butter, add ham. Mix together with the cheese and place in pie shells. Mix and pour over:

8 whole eggs
2 cups sour cream
2½ cups unwhipped, heavy cream
¾ teaspoon salt
1 teaspoon pepper
1 teaspoon nutmeg

Beat eggs 2 minutes on high. Mix sour cream with heavy cream. Add to eggs. Add salt, pepper and nutmeg. Pour over the ham and cheese filling. Bake at 375° between 30 and 35 minutes, or until firm.

CHEESE PALMIERS
Makes 4 dozen

1 pound puff paste
1 cup Parmesan cheese
1 tablespoon paprika
Egg wash

Roll out puff paste to 22" x 7", about ⅓-inch thick. Brush with egg and sprinkle Parmesan cheese, then paprika. Bring the wide sides (22") to the middle, then bring each wide side to the middle again. Fold in half lengthwise. The roll will be 1½" across and 22" long. Freeze 30 minutes. Slice ⅓" thick and bake flat on a paper-lined pan at 350° for 12 minutes.

BRIOCHE DOUGH

Makes 1 pound

Using the right bread flour is the key to light brioche and croissants, so try to find one from a specialty or natural food shop.

8 ounces high-gluten flour
8 ounces bread flour
⅓ cup plus 2 tablespoons granulated sugar
1½ teaspoons salt
1 ounce compressed yeast, crumbled
4 medium cold eggs
⅓ cup cold, whole milk
6 ounces unsalted butter, softened (If using salted butter, use
*   only 1 teaspoon salt in recipe.)*

Mix all ingredients except butter on second low speed for ten minutes, with a pastry hook attachment, or 15 minutes by hand, until paste is smooth and elastic. Be sure to keep ingredients cold; overmixing causes butter to melt. Butter and paste should have the same creamy consistency. Add the butter and mix for three minutes. Oil paste slightly and keep covered at room temperature until double in size.

Refrigerate 5 hours minimum or, better still, overnight. Dough can be frozen for more than one week, but will not be good longer than 36 hours in the refrigerator.

SMALL BRIOCHE ROLLS

Makes 10

1 pound brioche dough
Egg wash

Roll out dough and cut into 10 equal pieces. Roll each into a ball on a lightly floured surface. Put outer edge of your hand into flour and use it to make a small neck and head on each ball, rolling it with your hand. Grease muffin pan and press each ball into a cup, centering the head and pushing it down into the roll. Allow dough to rise uncovered for about an hour in a warm (not over 100°) place. Brush with egg wash and bake at 400° for around 12 minutes, or until golden brown.

BRIOCHE CINNAMON-PECAN COFFEE CAKE

1 pound brioche dough
1 cup pastry cream
¾ cup pecans
1 tablespoon sugar and ½ teaspoon cinnamon, mixed
Egg wash

Roll brioche dough into 15″ x 6″ rectangle. Smooth pastry cream over dough. Sprinkle pecans over cream, then sugar-cinnamon mixture. Roll up into a long roll as for sweet rolls. Cut into ten equal pieces. Arrange cut side down in 8″ x 1½″ cake pan, which has been well greased with margarine. Place one in the center and surround with eight. Flatten with hands and then let rise uncovered, to double in size to top of pan (temperature not over 100°). Note that dough is covered for its initial rising, but not after it is shaped. Bake at 400° for 8 minutes, then lower the temperature to 375° for 8 more minutes.

In the Adolphus pastry kitchen one muffin recipe produces 345 large muffins, which are then divided into three sets for the addition of flavoring. This recipe has been reduced from the original and, for that reason, makes 15 large muffins, rather than 12.

MUFFINS

Makes 15

½ cup butter, softened
¾ cup granulated sugar
2 whole eggs
1 tablespoon plus 1 teaspoon baking powder
2¼ cups sifted, all-purpose flour
1¼ cups milk
4 egg whites

Mix butter and sugar together for two minutes at medium speed. Add two whole eggs, one at a time, and mix one minute. Sift baking powder with flour and add alternately with milk to the mixture, beginning and ending with flour.

Mix two minutes, then add unbeaten eggwhites and mix two more minutes. The total beating time should not exceed eight minutes. At the last, add either:

3 teaspoons, vanilla, or
2½ teaspoons lemon extract, or
8 frozen blueberries per muffin.

For blueberry muffins, fill greased muffin cups half full with batter; place 4 berries in the center of each. Add batter to fill the cup to ¾ full, then, press 3 or 4 more berries on top. Cups should not be more than ¾ full. Bake muffins at 375° for 20 minutes, or until golden brown.

Baking bread can be a joy, if you have time to let the dough rise properly, and if you are willing to work with it until you master the technique of making it look appetizing. Certainly it helps to have a hook attachment to your mixer, but good bread can be mixed by hand.

Twist Bread gets its shine from being brushed with an egg wash. The extra step, which makes it beautiful, is a second wash right before baking. Add interest to the top with sesame or poppy seeds.

TWIST BREAD

Makes 1 large loaf and
1 medium loaf

6 cups high-gluten flour
1 tablespoon granulated sugar
1½ ounces compressed yeast
⅓ cup shortening
1 tablespoon salt
1 pint, plus ¼ cup ice water (18 ounces)
1 beaten egg, for wash
Poppy or sesame seeds (optional)

Mix all ingredients for 8 minutes with mixer hook, or about 15 minutes by hand, until the dough becomes smooth and elastic.

Form dough into a ball, covering surface lightly with either oil or the same flour you use in the recipe. Cover with plastic wrap or a damp cloth and let rise at room temperature for 30 minutes. At this point, dough may be refrigerated for 2-3 hours, if desired.

Divide dough into two parts. For the medium loaf, cut three 6-ounce pieces and roll each into a long roll with your hands. The other part should make three 10-ounce strips for the large loaf. Roll each strip separately to make the 10-ounce strips about 22" long and the 6-ounce strips, 18" long. Press three equal strips together at one end, pointing away from you. Braid to the end. Press ends together and tuck them under the loaf. Re-do the other end a little more tightly to give the loaf a nice shape.

Wash with egg and allow the loaves to rise again until doubled in size. Wash again with beaten egg; sprinkle with seeds. Bake at 400° for 20-25 minutes on a paper-lined sheet.

DANISH PASTRY   *Makes 7 dozen*

This seems to be a very large quantity; however, the dough can be frozen for up to a week before rolling or the Danish can be filled and frozen after baking. Cut the recipe in half, if it suits you better.

2 pounds, or 7½ cups high-gluten flour
¾ cups granulated sugar
2 teaspoons salt
½ cup dry yeast granules, or 2½ ounces compressed yeast
¼ pound unsalted butter
1¼ cups cold milk
5 medium eggs, cold
2 drops egg-yellow food color, or 2 yellow and ½ drop red

1¾ pounds soft butter
1 cup apricot marmalade to stick
Egg wash (1 beaten egg)

To Prepare: Mix first eight ingredients in mixer with hook attachment for ten minutes at medium speed, or by hand 15 minutes, until paste is smooth. Cover with clear plastic and let rise for 1-¼ hours.

Roll out paste about 17″ x 19″ in a rectangle on a floured board. Place soft butter in center. Fold 17″-edge, closest to you, to cover half the butter. Bring the opposite 17″ edge over to cover the other half. Fold the two ends on your right and left over to overlap slightly in the center of the dough. Refrigerate for 1 hour.

Roll out dough with the open side facing you. Make a double turn: Fold the edge farthest from you to the center of the dough, then fold the edge nearest you up to the same point. Fold the doubled edge nearest you over, bringing it to the center. Roll paste out again and roll-fold a single turn, bringing the farthest edge to the center, then folding the nearest edge up to meet it.

Refrigerate dough a minimum of 3 hours, or overnight. Or, freeze the dough up to a week before rolling into Danish pastries.

To Assemble: Roll out dough with flour. Do one more single turn, adding flour, and roll out 56 inches by 12½ inches. Unless you have a very long worktable, divide the pastry dough in two, and refrigerate one-half while working.

Spread one cup of apricot marmalade to make the pastry stick together. Cover the surface, leaving 1″ margin along the lower edge for egg wash. Brush on the egg. Start rolling over the top, and roll evenly all the way to the bottom edge, like a jelly roll. Place seam underneath and slice ½″ thick. Place on a paper-lined baking sheet two inches apart. Let rise in a warm place, 1½ hours minimum (about 90°, can be set close to open oven door).

Fill Danish by punching an indentation in the center and filling with any jam, marmalade or cherry pie filling. You can even use pastry cream filling, or make a Cheese Filling.

Cheese Filling

  1½ pounds cream cheese
  ½ cup granulated sugar
  1 tablespoon cornstarch
  1 egg, medium
  1 tablespoon vanilla

Mix cheese to soft texture. Add sugar and cornstarch. When smooth beat in whole egg and vanilla. Fill center of pastry.

For Pecan Danish, don't punch in the center. Brush with egg wash and sprinkle pecans only. Or brush with eggwash and sprinkle with 1 tablespoon cinnamon plus 2 tablespoons sugar.

Bake Danish at 400° for 15 minutes, or until golden brown. Remove from oven, cool 10 minutes and brush with apricot glaze to cover both pastry and filling or pecans.

If Danish are to be refrigerated or frozen for several days before baking, remove and thaw to room temperature before placing in warm place to rise on baking sheet. Then proceed as above by punching indentation in center, filling the dough and baking it.

OLD-FASHIONED BREAD   *Makes 2 1½ pound loaves*

4½ cups high-gluten flour
1 cup whole wheat flour
½ cup white rye flour
1 tablespoon plus ½ teaspoon salt
1 ounce compressed yeast
1 pint ice water
1 beaten egg, for wash

Mix all ingredients except egg for 8 minutes with the hook attachment of mixer, or by hand for 15 minutes, until smooth and elastic. Allow dough to rise 40 minutes at room temperature. Divide dough into two round loaves and work into doughnut shape. Do this by punching a hole with your elbow in the center of each. Catch it in the middle with one hand and roll it like a wheel with your hands grasping the inside. Even out the thickness all around so it will rise evenly.

Brush with egg wash and let rise until double in size. Just before baking, wash again with beaten egg. Sprinkle both loaves with ¼ cup of combined flours. Bake at 400° for 20 minutes, then reduce oven to 325° and continue baking for 8 minutes, or until crust is dry and crisp to touch.

Two Special Desserts

One of the smoothest, easiest desserts is a Caramel Custard or Flan. Since it has no nuts, chocolate or flour, this light taste treat can be eaten with minimum guilt.

CARAMEL CUSTARD

Makes 1 large flan or 10 small

Custard Mixture

1 quart milk
5 medium eggs
2 extra egg yolks
1½ cups granulated sugar
1 tablespoon vanilla

Scald the milk, and when it comes to a boil, remove the pan from the burner. Mix eggs, extra yolks, and sugar in a cold bowl. Add milk slowly to eggs and sugar. Strain and remove top film to make custard smooth. Set aside and make the caramel.

Caramel Mixture

1 cup sugar
½ cup water

Cook sugar and water in saucepan over medium heat, cleaning the side of the pan with a wet brush. When the mixture is golden brown, remove from flame and place saucepan in ice water to stop the heat immediately. Pour a thin layer on the bottom of the form. Freeze for 5 minutes to harden caramel. Add cooled egg mixture and cook in individual molds or a large flan mold set in a *bain marie*. Bake at 350° for 50 minutes. Test for firmness by touching center. Remove from hot water and cool completely. Refrigerate until serving (up to 5 days in the mold). Remove from mold by loosening edge with knife. Cover with plate and invert, shaking slightly to release.

GRAND MARNIER SOUFFLÉ GLACE *Makes 1 large mold or 10 small*

Prepare small molds as follows: Cut strips of aluminum foil 6" x 12", then fold double to 3" x 12". Brush the edge with shortening or butter to stick and wrap each strip around a rolling pin to make a mold 2½" in diameter. Fill the bottom of each with a piece of sponge cake. Make the syrup by bringing to a boil: ⅓ cup water and ¾ cup granulated sugar.

You need:

> 8 egg yolks
> 1 pint whipping cream, whipped soft
> 4 tablespoons Grand Marnier (other flavors can be used)

Whip yolks on medium speed and add warm syrup in a thin stream. Continue beating 10 minutes, until the mixture is light and fluffy and three times its original volume. Add Grand Marnier. (If desired, the mixture may be divided and flavored, such as one-half flavored with ⅓ cup melted chocolate, and half with ½ cup strawberry jam plus 2 or 3 drops lemon juice.) Fold whipped cream into mixture and spoon into molds. Freeze at least six hours before unmolding. May be served with fruit or sauce, or decorated with more whipped cream.

Ice Cream and Sherbet

In addition to baked desserts, the pastry kitchen of the Adolphus produces its own ice cream and sherbet. If you like to use your own ice cream freezer, you will enjoy trying some of these unusual flavors and imaginative combinations. The recipes vary only slightly, if you can make vanilla, you can make them all. The recipes have been reduced considerably from hotel proportions, but not changed. Compare the total amount of ingredients in each with the capacity of your own freezer in case you want to make more or less ice-cream.

VANILLA ICE CREAM

Makes 13-14 scoops

1 quart milk
1 cup plus 1 tablespoon granulated sugar
8 egg yolks
2 tablespoons vanilla extract
1 cup whipping cream (unwhipped)

Bring the milk to a boil. Meanwhile, beat egg yolks and granulated sugar for 5 minutes at high speed until very light in color. Change setting to low speed while adding 1 cup of the scalded milk. Return the mixture to the boiler and stir with a whisk until the mixture will coat a metal spoon. *Do not allow mixture to boil.* Remove it to another pan set in ice water to cool immediately (about 15 minutes). Strain and put mixture in ice-cream freezing machine. Mix 8-10 minutes until it becomes creamy smooth and thick. Add 2 tablespoons vanilla and fold in 1 cup of cream. Remove at once and place in deepfreeze.

CHOCOLATE-ORANGE ICE CREAM

Makes 13-14 scoops

1 quart milk
1 cup plus 1 tablespoon granulated sugar
8 egg yolks
½ cup plus 1 tablespoon melted, semisweet chocolate
3 tablespoons orange marmalade
3 teaspoons orange essence
Zest of two oranges
1 cup of unwhipped heavy cream

Follow the method for making Vanilla Ice Cream, substituting the chocolate for vanilla flavoring. Add the chocolate to the hot mixture before cooling over ice water. Continue the same method, adding the orange marmalade, essence and zest just before the cream is added at the last. Remove from freezer and place in deepfreeze for storage.

CHESTNUT ICE CREAM

1 quart milk
8 egg yoks
1 cup sugar
1 cup chestnut spread (available in specialty shops)
4 tablespoons rum
1 cup whipping cream

Follow Vanilla method except, in place of vanilla, fold in rum mixed with chestnut spread before adding cream.

HONEY ICE CREAM

1 quart milk
8 egg yolks
1 cup sugar
1 cup honey
1 cup heavy cream

Follow the procedure for making Vanilla Ice Cream. As soon as the milk comes to a boil, add ½ cup of the honey. Before adding the thick, unwhipped cream, add the other half-cup of honey.

ALMOND ICE CREAM

1 quart milk
8 egg yolks
1 cup plus 1 tablespoon granulated sugar
¾ cup sliced almonds, roasted dry in a low oven
1 tablespoon almond extract
1 cup whipping cream

Follow the vanilla recipe, leaving out the vanilla extract. Add almonds and extract right at the last. Fold in the cream and store in the deepfreeze.

RUM-RAISIN ICE CREAM

1 quart milk
8 egg yolks
1 cup plus 1 tablespoon granulated sugar
1 cup heavy cream, unwhipped
1 cup raisins
⅓ cup rum
3 tablespoons rum to flavor ice cream

The day before making ice cream, rinse raisins and dry with a cloth. Leave them to soak in a bowl with ⅓ cup rum for 24 hours to soften and flavor the raisins. Follow the Vanilla Ice Cream directions. Before adding the cream, add the raisins and 3 tablespoons rum. Mix briefly, then add cream and continue to beat till mixed. Store in deepfreeze.

If you want to add an impressive touch to a dinner party, try serving one of these between-courses ices to clear the palate during the meal. They are semisweet, as served in the French Room.

CHAMPAGNE SHERBET   *Makes ½ gallon*

2¾ cups water
2¾ cups granulated sugar
1 bottle champagne
1 cup lemon juice, freshly squeezed

Make a syrup by bringing sugar and water to a boil. Add the lemon juice and cool. Put the mixture in the freezing machine and mix until it begins to set. Add the champagne and continue freezing in the machine until smooth. Remove and store in deepfreeze.

White Wine Sherbet can be made in a similar way. Substitute a liter bottle of white wine for the champagne and increase the lemon juice to 1 cup plus 2 tablespoons.

LEMON SHERBET   *Makes 12-14 scoops*

2¾ cups water
2¾ cups granulated sugar
2 cups fresh lemon juice
2 cups water for the lemon juice

Make a syrup by bringing sugar and water to a boil. Add the lemon juice and water and cool. Put the mixture in the machine and freeze until smooth.

GRAPEFRUIT SHERBET   *Makes 12-14 scoops*

8 cups freshly squeezed grapefruit juice
2 cups plus 5 tablespoons granulated sugar
½ cup dry vermouth

Strain grapefruit juice. Add sugar and stir until dissolved, then add vermouth. Do not heat. Put the mixture in the machine and freeze until smooth.

Once you start making sherbets, you might adopt them as a part of your home entertaining favorites. Health and fitness trends have prompted many gourmets to reconcile their taste for rich desserts to simple sherbet, thus leaving the major calorie consumption for the meal itself. Another advantage is that sherbet can be kept on hand, melted, and then refrozen in the machine. Storing several flavors enables you to combine two or three small scoops in a dish for a variety of colors and flavors (add an Almond Tuile or two, and pour liqueur or vodka over the sherbet, if you want a class act). To make good sherbet, use exactly the recommended proportions in the recipes. Save experimentation for serving combinations.

Two special sherbets are made without the syrup, using sugar and fruit: Raspberry Sherbet and Kiwi Sherbet. Layering the two in a mold or a bowl produces a conversation-stopping dessert. Decorate it with fresh fruit and/or whipped cream. Beware, though . . . it's expensive!

RASPBERRY SHERBET

Makes 1 quart

1 quart fresh raspberry puree, made with 6 1-pint boxes raspberries
1 cup sugar
2 tablespoons lemon juice

Blend raspberries and press through sieve three times. Add sugar and lemon juice and freeze the mixture in the machine until smooth. To make layered dessert, line a bowl with the raspberry sherbet, cover with clear plastic and freeze while you make the next layer:

KIWI SHERBET

Makes 1 quart

3 cups kiwi fruit, pureed in blender (about 25)
¾ cups dry vermouth
1 cup sugar
2 tablespoons lemon juice

Puree the kiwi fruit, the number it takes to make 3 cups. Add dry vermouth, sugar and lemon juice. Sieve twice to take out the seeds. Put the mixture in the machine and freeze until smooth.

To Assemble: Remove plastic wrap from raspberry sherbet bowl and fill with Kiwi Sherbet. Place a plastic wrap over all of it and store in the deepfreeze until very firm. Unmold and slice: serve garnished with fresh fruit and if desired, a dollop of whipped cream . . . but the fruit is enough.

A Less Expensive Idea: Use either the raspberry or kiwi to line the mold, then fill with one of the other flavors of sherbet (a different color). Remember that the raspberry and kiwi recipes make only half as much as the other sherbet recipes in this collection.

PEAR WILLIAMS SHERBET

Makes ½ gallon

5 cups of canned pears pureed in blender
1 cup pear juice
4 tablespoons fresh lemon juice
1¾ cups sugar
1¾ cups water
4 tablespoons Pear Williams Liqueur

Bring sugar and water to a boil. Remove from flame and add puree, pear juice and lemon juice. Cool and place in the machine; freeze only until set. Add the liqueur and continue freezing until smooth. Store in deepfreeze.

APPLE CALVADOS SHERBET

Makes ½ gallon

4 cups unsweetened apple juice
3 cups water
2¾ cups sugar
1 cup plus 2 tablespoons Calvados liqueur

Bring the water and sugar to a boil to make the syrup. Add the apple juice and cool. Put mixture in the machine to freeze until set. Add the Calvados and continue freezing until smooth.

PINEAPPLE SHERBET

Makes ½ gallon

2¾ cups water
2¾ cups sugar
1 cup pineapple juice (canned, not from crushed pineapple)
2 cups crushed pineapple, drained
1 tablespoon Kirsch

Make the syrup by bringing the water and sugar to a boil. Add pineapple juice and the drained, crushed pineapple. Cool, add Kirsch, then freeze until smooth in the machine.

LIME SHERBET

Makes ½ gallon

Use both lemon and lime juices to make this one. Using only lime leaves a bitter taste which can't be corrected satisfactorily with sugar.

1 cup freshly squeezed lime juice
1 cup fresh lemon juice
2 cups water
2¾ cups water
2¾ cups sugar
2 drops green food color

Bring the water and sugar to a boil to make the syrup. Add other ingredients and cool. Freeze in machine until smooth.

STRAWBERRY SHERBET

Makes ½ gallon

4 pints fresh strawberries, or enough to make 5 cups puree
2 cups granulated sugar
2⅓ cups water
¼ cup fresh lemon juice
2 tablespoons strawberry flavoring

Make syrup by bringing to a boil the sugar and water. Wash and hull strawberries and puree in blender. Mash puree through a sieve to remove seeds. Fold fresh strawberry puree and lemon juice into syrup mixture. Allow to cool to room temperature. Put into freezer machine to freeze until smooth.

ORANGE SHERBET

Makes ½ gallon

4 cups fresh orange juice
3 tablespoons lemon juice, freshly squeezed
1 cup plus 2 tablespoons sugar
1 cup water

Make the sugar syrup by bringing water and sugar to a boil. Add orange juice and lemon juice. Cool to room temperature. Put into the machine and freeze until smooth.

Decorating

You may have fixed ideas about using natural, edible garnishes for your buffet trays: ruffled lettuce, cherry tomatoes, olives, pickled beets, spiced peaches, etc. However, if you want to give your designs added flair, try setting a design in aspic such as the one shown on page 76, which is made with leek leaves and flower petals for a fine line design.

Michel Cornu recommends using other things for a less formal buffet tray. Create a western scene with cactus cut from asparagus, a setting orange-peel sun and distant birds made of slivered leek leaves or bell pepper splinters. Practice cutting designs before you start setting in a pattern. Try looking at everything you have used for garnish as a possibility. Black olives, pimiento, carrots, lemons, beets, and spiced peaches all lend color. Likewise, mushrooms, green olives, hearts of artichoke or palm can all be pared into designs. Here's how Michel does it:

Dissolve 1 ounce of plain, unflavored gelatin in ¼ cup cold water. Add to 2¼ cups milk. Stir over low heat until the jelly mixture is completely melted and dissolved . . . do not boil. Allow to cool at room temperature until jelly starts to set. Cover the entire bottom of a tray with a thin layer of aspic, being sure to press out any bubbles. Refrigerate tray until the congealed mixture is firm.

Blanch leek leaves three or four minutes in boiling water. Remove and cool. Cut into stems, graceful arcs, leaves, or some geometrical pattern, if you prefer. An aspic cutter, bought in a cooking specialty store, helps you to cut dainty shapes from real flower petals. Use bright flowers . . . red, yellow, purple . . . for best results, rather than pastels. When satisfied with the design, dissolve another ounce of unflavored gelatin in ¼ cup cold water. Add 2¼ cups water. Heat mixture until gelatin is dissolved. Do not boil. Allow to cool until nearly set. Press design slightly onto aspic-lined tray. Pour a thin layer of the second gelatin mixture over carefully, removing any bubbles. Refrigerate until firm.

Beautifully decorated cakes in the pastry kitchen are the result of simple, edible additions. These favorites are used in many different combinations:

Strawberries, halved or whole
Sliced kiwi
Thin slices of lemon, lime and orange
Whole raspberries
Melted chocolate (or set in molds)
Red jam, any kind
Apricot jam
Crystallized violets
Apricot Glaze
Whipped cream
Tiny choux swans
Butter Cream

Set your mind to improving the looks of desserts, if they lack color. Apricot Glaze adds a shiny finish to almost everything from lemon tart to Danish pastry. Butter Cream and jam (red or apricot) lend themselves to effective decorating on the cake plate or tray as well as on the cake.

The Nouvelle Cakes especially need something to boost their color, even though they are served with a sauce. Try slicing kiwi fruit very thin and fitting the slices all around the edge, with half of each slice over the top edge and half down the side. Pipe a Butter Cream edge around the resulting scalloped ring, and a tiny stripe of red jam, if you like. Learn to pipe decorative patterns, even if you limit your piping to outlining simple shapes. Use your imagination and your own favorite color schemes.

A novel way to serve petits fours and other teatime dainties also comes from the pastry kitchen: a Nougatine Tray. Boxes and baskets are possible, too, if you are patient and measure carefully. But the tray can be made by anyone. Use a lacy gold doily to make it festive.

NOUGATINE TRAY

To make a 12″ round or square tray prepare a work surface as you would for toffee. Oiled marble is best, but whatever you use, oil it; don't use flour. It could be a counter top or a cutting board. Oil a spatula or palette, as well, and a baking sheet.

3 cups plus 1 tablespoon granulated sugar
⅓ cup corn syrup
4 cups almond slices, with skins left on

Heat the corn syrup, add the sugar and cook 5 or 6 minutes, stirring and turning constantly until the mixture is a light caramel color. Remove immediately. Add almonds and mix into a paste. Pour out on an oiled baking sheet which has been heated. Leave in a 250° oven five minutes to keep the mixture soft. For a mold, cover the back side of a tray with foil, then oil the foil. Roll out almond mixture quickly on the oiled surface. Place the inverted tray on it and cut the nougatine to measure. Then fit the cut nougatine onto the back of the tray and shape it over the foil.

When nougatine is cold, remove tray and foil. If you want to pipe a border around it, here's a good, firm one:

1½ cup powdered sugar
1 egg white

Mix five minutes with a palette or spatula; add food coloring, if desired. Pipe around the edge for decoration.

NOUGATINE CANDY

The nougatine mixture above is edible, but not good as candy. If you want to make candy nougatine, add 1 tablespoon melted butter to the almonds, and ½ cup heavy cream. Roll out the mixture and cut into bars, 2″ x 1″. Dip one end into melted chocolate.

The Banquet Kitchen

Perhaps the best time to snoop into the Adolphus' kitchens is right before a banquet or a big party. A single peek through a fish-eye lens would reveal all of them in motion at once. In one part, an ice-sculpture might be in the making; on another side, a flower design might be settling into an aspic glaze on a tray; fresh fruit might be soaking in vats of orange juice, while cheese arrangements and slices of páte may have been formed into a pattern on a large, framed mirror. From the separate kitchens a striking array is assembled in the serving kitchen adjoining the Grand Ballroom. Banquet Chef Filbert Johnson puts it all together.

Depending on the size and formality of the occasion, the selection might include a number of recipes in this collection. From the French Room kitchen, one might find Vegetable Terrine, Seafood Ballottine, and Rack of Lamb Persillade. Any of the soups from the Grille could be served: Cold Cucumber, Lobster Bisque, Clam Chowder, or Baked Onion Soup. A brunch might reveal Eggs Sardou, or steamed vegetables with herbed butter, or colorful, cold salads.

Cocktail parties can be beautiful affairs. One of the popular ways to serve from long tables in the ballroom can be scaled and adapted to your home. The Adolphus uses large, framed mirrors to serve slices of pate, Seafood Ballottine and Vegetable Terrine, and small quiche squares, either the Lorraine or a variation substituting broccoli tops, zucchini and yellow squash slices for the ham.

VOL-AU-VENTS MAISON

For receptions, Vol-au-Vents Maison remain the preferred traditional fare. To make them, fill small Vol-au-Vents (see

Pastry section . . . or buy them) with a mixture of:

> *3 pounds diced chicken, cooked*
> *1 quart cream*
> *1 pint Béchamel Sauce*
> *¼ cup sherry*
> *Salt and pepper*

Reduce cream, Béchamel and sherry to half-volume. Add chicken. The mixture should be thick, the consistency of mincemeat pie filling.

If you like to do cold buffets at home, borrow this idea from Filbert Johnson about serving: Fill a big, aluminum foil or metal steam pan with ice, bank greenery around it to hide the pan, and set your cold buffet bowls down in the ice. Make the ice look pretty, too, with greenery, flowers, or edible, colorful decorations. Fill pretty glass bowls with:

FRESH FRUIT SALAD

> *Fresh pineapple*
> *Both red and green apples*
> *Black and purple grapes*
> *Fresh cantaloupe*
> *Honeydew melon*
> *Anything else*

Soak apples in water and lemon juice briefly (proportion is ½ gallon water to ¼ cup lemon juice). Stir well and leave apples to soak a short time. Drain and soak them in orange juice with the other fruit. Store fruit in orange juice, if necessary.

To Serve: line a bowl with leaf lettuce, and fill with drained fruit. Decorate the top with whatever you have: a pineapple top can be used, or a rose made by paring a thin skin of apple, orange or lemon in one long, twirling strip. Roll it up and invert it to look like a rose. Halved strawberries and mint leaves make a nice finish, too.

These two cold buffet recipes are best made the simple, old fashioned way.

SIMPLY CHICKEN SALAD   *Serves 20*

5 pounds of cooked chicken, boned and diced
1 whole celery bunch, without leaves, diced
1 pint mayonnaise
Salt, pepper, onion, or onion salt, if desired
A few bell pepper strips for color

POTATO SALAD VINAIGRETTE   *Serves 20*

5 pounds small, new potatoes, quartered
¾ pound bacon, about 12 slices
2 bunches scallions
Salt and pepper
Salad oil and red vinegar, to moisten completely

Steam potatoes about 8-10 minutes, with skins left on. Fry and chop bacon, or use ½ pound prepared bacon bits. Chop scallions, using the green part as well as the white. Add salt and pepper to taste, and oil and red vinegar.

With cold buffets, serve one hot thing, such as a big tureen of soup, if possible, and Cheese Straws or Cheese Palmiers (see *Pastry* section) or these:

CHEESE PUFFS   *Makes 5 dozen*

1 pound Choux Paste
1 cup Swiss cheese, grated
1 teaspoon pepper
1 teaspoon salt
1 teaspoon paprika
1 egg for brushing tops

Begin with choux paste at room temperature. Mix everything except the egg together and drop by tablespoon, elongating them into eclair shape, onto a baking sheet lined with plain white paper. Brush with beaten egg and bake at 375° for 15 minutes. The uncooked mixture keeps four days in the refrigerator, but must be softened to room temperature before baking.

If the buffet is a brunch, the Danish Rolls make a good show, but the Brioche Cinnamon-Pecan Coffee Cake is the sought-after unusual. With any party, the sweet pastry tarts are a good dessert, especially if filled with lemon, but any flavored cheesecake, or Apple Tarts are also wonderful with coffee. For a birthday, go all out with the Chocolate Meringue Icing-topped Marble Birthday Cake. Or, if you can keep them long enough to serve (hide them): Chocolate Truffles. Any cake or sherbet in this collection adds a nice finish to a party.

Surprise your dinner party guests with an interesting color-stack cake dessert. Split one white layer and one chocolate layer and stack them with different color-flavors of Perfect Filling. Frost with the chocolate flavored Butter Cream Frosting.

Mixing colors and flavors opens a whole new world of ideas. Try mixing several shades of ice cream scoops, or sherbet. Layer them in molds to serve with Pound Cake, or with sauce, or both.

The possibilities for entertaining are endless, adding the Adolphus' semi-European-Texas hospitality to a good measure of your own.

Glossary

AL DENTE: Cooking pasta or vegetables to a firm but tender stage.

À LA BOURGUIGNONNE: In the style of Burgundy, usually cooked in red wine.

ASSIETTE DE LA FERME: "A plate from the farm"; in this recipe, a serving of game birds.

BAIN MARIE: A large pan, or "bath," in which to keep a pan of food warm, or to cook it slowly without exposing to direct heat. This larger relative of the double boiler is filled with water so a pan sitting in it is covered half way up the sides.

BALLOTTINE: Dish made from boned poultry, meat or fish, stuffed and pressed into a symmetrical shape and served hot or cold.

BLANCH: To plunge into boiling water for the purpose of softening a food, or for partial cooking or precooking.

BOUQUET GARNI: A combination of herbs, usually parsley, thyme and bay leaf, tied together during cooking and removed before serving.

CUISSES DE GRENOUILLES: "Cruisses de grenouilles au parfum de Provençe" — frog legs with the flavor of Provençe.

DEGLAZE: To remove most of the fat from a cooked dish and add stock or wine to make a thin sauce from the brown bits remaining in the pan.

FEUILLANTINE DE RIS DE VEAU: Veal sweetbreads served on puff pastry.

FLAMBE: Flamed by pouring cognac or other liqueur over food, lighting and allowing the alcohol to burn away.

GRATIN: A dish with a browned top crust, usually a sauced dish topped with crumbs or cheese and placed under the broiler.

GRENADIN DE VEAU AUX CHANTERELLES: Small slices of veal fillet with chanterelles, a mushroom in the shape of a cup with a frilly edge and thick swollen gills the color of egg yolk.

HARICOTS VERT: Green beans

JULIENNE: Thin matchlike strips

MARINADE: A seasoned liquid, cooked or uncooked, in which food is steeped.

MIREPOIX: Finely diced onion, carrot and celery cooked slowly in butter and seasonings. Used as flavoring.

MOUSSE: An aspic of pureed fish or meat, sometimes vegetables. Any light dessert containing beaten egg whites or whipped cream.

PERIGOURDINE (à la): Any dish including a garnish of truffles.

PERSILLADE: The term for chopped parsley, sometimes mixed with garlic and added to dishes at the end of cooking.

POACH: To simmer gently in liquid.

POULET: Chicken

PUREE: Sieved or ground into a fine pulp.

TERRINE: Oblong earthenware dish similar to bread tin. Also denotes food cooked in this type of dish.

TIMBALE: From the Arab "thabal" meaning "drum"; a food made in a plain round mold with high sides.

TOURNEDOS SAUTE AUX TRUFFES: Small slices of beef fillet sautéed with truffles.

ZEPHIR GRENOUILLES: A light preparation made with frog legs.

ZEST: The exterior, colored, flavored part of the skin of citrus.

Index